# Counterresistance

# Counterresistance: The Therapist's Interference with the Therapeutic Process

Gerald Schoenewolf, Ph.D.

**JASON ARONSON INC.**
*Northvale, New Jersey*
*London*

The author gratefully acknowledges permission to reprint chapters of this book that have previously been published elsewhere. Chapters 2 and 12 appeared in *Voices: The Art and Science of Psychotherapy*. Chapter 2, "To See Without Seeking," appeared in volume 28, no. 4, copyright © 1993, and Chapter 12, "The Uses of Objective Counterresistance," appeared in modified form as "Difficult Patients I Have Known and Hated," in volume 27, no. 4, copyright © 1992. Both are reprinted with permission of the American Academy of Psychotherapists, and the Guilford Press. Chapter 11, "Emotional Contagion," appeared in *Modern Psychoanalysis*, volume 15, no. 1, copyright © 1990 and is reprinted here by permission of the Center for Modern Psychoanalytic Studies.

This book was set in 11 pt. Goudy by Lind Graphics of Upper Saddle River, New Jersey, and printed and bound by Haddon Craftsmen of Scranton, Pennsylvania.

**Library of Congress Cataloging-in-Publication Data**

Schoenewolf, Gerald.
    Counterresistance / by Gerald Schoenewolf.
      p.   cm.
    Includes bibliographical references and index.
    ISBN 1-56821-079-5 (hard cover)
    1. Resistance (Psychoanalysis)  2. Countertransference
(Psychology)  I. Title.
    [DNLM:  1. Defense Mechanisms.  2. Psychoanalytic Therapy.
3. Countertransference (Psychology)  WM 460 S365c 1993]
RC489.R49S36   1993
616.89'17—dc20
DNLM/DLC
for Library of Congress                93-17264

Manufactured in the United States of America. Jason Aronson Inc. offers books and cassettes. For information and catalog write to Jason Aronson Inc., 230 Livingston Street, Northvale, New Jersey 07647.

To Richard Robertiello, M.D.

# Contents

# Tables and Figures

# Preface

Although there is no lack of literature on resistance, there is hardly any literature on counterresistance. A few authors writing on technique have called attention to the importance of counterresistance, but most either do not mention it at all or merely give it lip service. For example, Greenson (1967) devotes only a few paragraphs to it. He, like most others, concentrates almost all his attention on matters of analyzing transference and resistance; that is, he focuses almost entirely on the patient's psychodynamics.

This book advances a perhaps radical proposition: that the first and foremost responsibility of psychotherapists is to analyze their own resistances. Once therapists have analyzed and resolved their own resistances to their patients, the rest will follow. This holds true for novices as well as seasoned professionals, for we never outgrow our resistances entirely, and each new patient offers a new challenge. Moreover, it is my contention that in most cases, therapeutic failures result not from the inability of analysts to analyze and resolve patients' resistances, but from their failure to analyze and resolve their own. Finally, I also contend that this emphasis by therapists on analyzing the patient precludes one of the primary means of bringing about change. Change and cure are brought about through the relationship itself, and psychotherapists who analyze their patients but not themselves risk being like those parents who say, "Do as I say, not as I do." Therapists must show through both word and deed how a healthy personality functions; they must set an example for the patient by showing the patient that they are aware of their own resistances. Therefore, the first question the therapist must ask at every moment in a session is, "How am *I* resisting now?"

The therapy relationship, like every dyad, is reciprocal: Every thought by the patient begets a counterthought by the therapist; every impulse a counterimpulse; every action a counteraction. At the same time, every thought by the therapist begets a counterthought by the patient; every impulse a counterimpulse; every action a counteraction. It is an ongoing dance of resistance and counterresistance. You cannot have one without the other.

This book is intended as a primer for psychotherapists, delineating the kinds of counterresistances, how they manifest themselves, and how to analyze and resolve them.

# 1

# Resistance and Counterresistance

A certain patient keeps coming late for his sessions. He is an angry young man who largely disowns his anger and acts it out in this and other ways.

The therapist, an older man, at first gently brings up the lateness almost as an afterthought, hoping the patient will take the hint and begin talking about it of his own accord. He does not. Then the therapist starts to call it to the patient's attention more rigorously.

"You know, you're always about 10 minutes late."

"Is it that much?"

"Yes, about 10 minutes."

"That's interesting. I never thought about it."

"Well, now that you're thinking about it, what do you think it means?"

3

"I don't know. What do you think it means?"

"I haven't the slightest."

"Neither do I."

"You're the one who comes late."

"You're the shrink."

Trying to get the patient to analyze this resistance went nowhere. So he silently analyzed it, noting that the patient had a harsh, punitive father and a teasing older brother, that he seemed fixated in the anal stage (anal withholding), that his mother had been quite withholding of affection toward him, and that he had not been allowed in his family to express feelings directly. He noted furthermore that the patient had a characterological disposition to be late—that he was chronically late for work, school, and practically everything else. After analyzing all this silently, he began giving the patient interpretations. "I think you come late because you think I'm going to be like the people in your family, harsh and strict like your father, teasing like your brother, withholding like your mother." The patient nodded and begrudgingly agreed with the interpretations, but he continued to come late. As time passed the therapist became exasperated, but he hid this feeling from the patient and even, to an extent, from himself. Finally, he could do so no longer.

"I don't understand why you keep coming late, " the therapist proclaimed one day with a certain gravity.

"You sound angry."

"What if I am?"

"Why should I come on time, when you're not really here yourself?" the patient snapped.

"What do you mean?"

"I just don't think you're really here. You're always hiding back there behind your blank screen."

It was when the therapist came out from hiding, when he revealed his true emotions by expressing his exasperation through his tone of his voice, that the patient finally began to talk. The patient had put his finger on the real problem. The real problem was not the patient's resistance, but the therapist's.

This therapist, like many therapists, had taken the concept of the "blank screen" and used it as a rationale to hide his own fear of intimacy. In fact, he had a counterresistance stemming from several sources. First of all there was a countertransference resistance to the patient. From the moment the patient entered his office, he was reminded of his father, who often had a sulky expression similar to the patient's, and he anticipated that if he were not careful the patient might become cold and rejecting like his father. He had, in fact, transferred his relationship with his father onto the patient, and he became extra guarded whenever the patient came for a session. In doing so, he unconsciously baited the patient into becoming cold and rejecting so that he could return to his own fixation point, relive his repeating pattern, and try to make it right this time.

At the same time the therapist also had a characterological resistance to intimacy. He had been an only child of working parents and had suffered a great deal of emotional deprivation in his childhood. His conscious reason for being a therapist was to achieve the intimate contact he had lacked as a child; unconsciously he emotionally distanced his patients in exactly the way his parents had distanced him. The blank screen suited him perfectly, matching up with his characterological disposition toward emotional distance.

Finally, the therapist's resistance was also fueled by ideology, and was therefore a cultural resistance as well. It was reinforced by the ideology of psychoanalysis, namely the concepts of the blank screen and abstinence. In other words, this resistance was also bred by the culture in which he lived and specifically by the psychoanalytic doctrine of that culture. Indeed, it was this cultural counterresistance that was most crucial in prolonging the impasse, since it became the "scientific"—hence unquestionable—rationale for the resistance.

Since the therapist was unconscious of his own resistance, he could not resolve the patient's resistance. Instead of questioning the patient about his lateness or making interpretations, he might have asked, "What am *I* doing wrong to cause you to come late?" Then the patient would have felt free to verbalize negative feelings about the therapist or to look at himself without feeling put on the spot.

The concepts of the blank screen and abstinence have, I believe, been misunderstood by psychoanalysts and analytic therapists. The blank screen does not mean that the therapist should be a technician, totally devoid of any normal human traits. Abstinence does not mean that a therapist should be completely unresponsive to the patient.

Rather, the blank screen simply requires that the therapist not gratuitously blab out details of his own life that are not necessary for the patient to know, which might at some point give the patient a hook to hang his own resistances on. And abstinence means simply that the therapist does not attempt to gratify his own needs through the patient.

The patient is required to split his ego, letting one part observe while the other part is free to verbalize all thoughts and feelings. The therapist must in fact do likewise. His observing ego allies itself with the patient's, and his participating ego feels all the feelings and thinks all the thoughts aroused by the therapy dyad. He does not attempt to hide those feelings and thoughts from the patient or from himself, and at times he must be prepared to verbalize them. It is only when the therapist is completely there at an emotional, participatory level with the patient, when he has given up his own defenses and is not resisting intimacy, that the patient can come out of his defensive posture. The therapist must take the lead.

This concept of an emotionally involved therapist who at the same time maintains an observing ego is not new. It has existed from the beginning of psychoanalysis. Indeed, the first analyst, Josef Breuer (Breuer and Freud 1893–1895), was quite emotionally responsive to his patient, Anna O., and for this reason the therapy relationship became intense. Unfortunately, Breuer could not maintain an observing ego, nor did he remain abstinent in the true meaning of that term; instead he fell in love with the patient and began to gratify his own emotional needs, making this patient his whole life, visiting her at her home twice a day, seven days a week, to the neglect of his own wife and family.

Other therapists have since refined this way of doing therapy (Balint 1968, Ferenczi 1930, Fromm-Reichmann 1950, Reich 1933, Searles 1979, Spotnitz 1985, Winnicott 1947). Today, even the most traditional analysts concede that therapists must be capable of responding to the particular requirements of different patients, be they neurotics, narcissists, borderlines, or psychotics. Yet, while making this concession, many still fail to recognize the importance of analyzing their counterresistances, and their emotional involvement with their patients remains subjective.

In Freud's day, psychoanalysts, including Freud, harbored the notion that they were more or less well and patients were sick, and hence they concentrated almost entirely on analyzing the patient. If a therapist had erotic or aggressive feelings about a patient, these were considered a potential hazard that Freud urged therapists to "overcome" (1910, p. 145). Since then there has been a shift in the thinking of the analytic community. It is recognized that we therapists should be more advanced than our patients, due to our own therapy and supervision, but we are all the products of less than perfect childhoods and we can never completely work through our psychopathlogy. Therefore, we no longer see ourselves as well and our patients as unwell, but rather our patients are a little less well than we are, and it is our responsibility to analyze both our own and the patients' resistances. It seems almost axiomatic that therapists must analyze and resolve their own resistances ("Physician, heal thyself!") before they can analyze and resolve the resistances of their patients.

## HISTORY OF THE CONCEPTS

In analytic literature, resistance refers to the way in which a patient defends against potential dangers inherent in relating to the therapist. Freud (1900) defined it as "whatever interrupts the progress" (p. 517), and wrote of "defenses" and "resistances" synonymously (1912, 1914, 1926, 1937). Patients resist the therapeutic procedure, the therapist, and their own healthy needs for closeness and release. They defend the neurotic guilt, the narcissistic grandiosity, the borderline fear, the psychotic rage. They defend against merger, dependency, incorporation, and loss of self. They resist being smothered, manipulated, deprived, violated, abused, driven crazy. And, yes, they resist finding out about their resistances. Therapists can have all of these same resistances— although, it is hoped, to a lesser degree.

Resistances have been classified in various ways by various authors. Freud (1926) and Glover (1955) classified them according to the source of the resistance, be it ego, id, or superego, or by fixation point—does the resistance stem from a fixation in the oral, anal, or phallic stage? A. Freud (1936) classified them according to types of defense, such as repression, isolation, projection, displacement, and reaction formation. Others have classified them according to diagnostic category: hysterical resistance, obsessional resistance, borderline resistance, narcissistic resistance.

There is some confusion regarding the classifications of resistances. For example, Freud's delineation of four types—ego, id, superego, and transference resistances—was confusing because the first three are related to source, while the latter has to do with the patient–therapist dyad. There has also been a debate over whether the terms *defense* and *resistance* are indeed synonymous, as Freud posited. Gill (1982), for example, sees defenses as intrapsyhic (characterological) and resistances as interpersonal (transferential). However, I think this is just another way of saying that there are two types of resistances—defensive (characterological) and interpersonal (transferential)—which happens to be the way I have chosen to classify them. Then there is confusion about the terms *transference resistance* and *resistance*. Although Freud did not think that resistance was always part of the transference, others, such as Gill, believe that "resistance can be expressed only in the transference" (1982, p. 33). However, while Gill sees all resistance as transference, he does not view all transference as resistance. He makes a distinction between transference of wishes and transference of defense, following Freud (1912), who referred to the transference of wishes as a positive transference that facilitated the forming of the therapeutic alliance and was therefore not resistance.

I disagree with the assertion that all resistance is an expression of transference. In my own system of classification, I posit a cultural resistance that springs not from childhood conditioning but from circumstances in society at the time of the therapy that impinge on the therapy (See Chapter 6), and this resistance has mainly to do with defenses, such as projection and splitting, rather than with transference.

While reams have been written about analyzing resistance, the literature on analyzing counterresistance is sparse. Freud first took note of it in 1910, remarking that "we have noticed that no psycho-analyst goes further than his own complexes and internal resistances permit" (p. 145). Ferenczi and Rank (1925) alluded to it indirectly, pointing out that

> the narcissism of the analyst seems suited to create a particularly fruitful source of mistakes, among others the development of a narcissistic countertransference which provokes the patient into pushing into the foreground certain things which flatter the analyst and on the other hand, into suppressing remarks and associations of an unpleasant nature in relation to him. [p. 41]

Jung (1935) noted that the analytic process was a "reciprocal reaction of two psychic systems" (p. 4). Fromm-Reichmann (1950) devoted a chapter to counterresistance, although she did not call it such, and alluded to cultural counterresistance when she noted, "the recovery of many schizophrenics and schizoid personalities . . . depends upon the psychotherapist's freedom from convention and prejudice" (p. 32). Glover (1955) stated, "If analysts maintain, as they do maintain, that during the transference neurosis everything the patient thinks, says or does can, if necessary or expedient, be interpreted as transference, then surely everything the analyst thinks, says or does during the countertransference can, where necessary or expedient, be self-interpreted as counterresistance" (p. 98).

Racker (1968) considers various kinds of counterresistance, but his notion is primarily concerned with instances in which psychoanalysts, due to identification with the patient, unconsciously join the patient's resistance, thus the term *counter—* meaning corresponding—*resistance.* (He coined the term complementary identification.) Greenson (1967) mentions counterresistance only in one paragraph, more or less parroting Racker's definition. "It is important . . . not to play into the resistance of the patient by using the same kind of resistance he does" (p. 123).

Spotnitz (1985) emphasizes the roles of countertransference resistance in working with schizophrenic patients. Noting that it is hard enough for a fairly well-analyzed therapist to tolerate the strong emotions such patients induce when they are in a state of narcissistic transference, he asserts that it is even harder if the therapist has characterological problems. "A strong and well-integrated ego is essential to function well analytically with psychotic patients and to control one's behavior under the impact of the feelings they induce" (p. 240). Spotnitz lists three major sources of countertransference resistance: the need not to feel hate, the need to be liked, and the need to be right.

I have introduced yet another way of classi-

fying resistances and counterresistances (Robertiello and Schoenewolf 1987) and have proposed a
new category of resistance that I dubbed *cultural
resistances*. As the opening vignette illustrates,
there are three types of resistance under my
schema: transference and countertransference
resistances, which are aroused specifically by
the transference–countertransference relationship;
characterological resistances and counterresistances, which are the characteristic way a patient or
therapist resists closeness in and out of the therapy
office; and cultural resistances and counterresistances, which stem from the wider influences of the
culture in which a patient or therapist lives. Sometimes, as in my opening vignette, a patient or therapist can be influenced by all three types of resistance at the same time. Sometimes it's only one type
of resistance.

I make a further distinction between objective
and subjective resistances and counterresistances.
Objective resistances and counterresistances are
those that are provoked by the therapist or patient
and have little or nothing to do with transferential,
characterological, or cultural factors. For example,
a therapist may arrive late for a patient's first
session due to some real and unavoidable circum-
stance—maybe because the subway stalled. Subsequently, the patient may have difficulty opening up
or trusting the therapist in this first session. This
would be a normal reaction; hence, it would be
objective resistance. It would be provoked entirely
by the real relationship with the therapist and have
little or nothing to do with the patient's transference to the therapist, characterological predisposi-

tions, or cultural biases. Similarly, patients may provoke objective resistances (or impulses to resist) in therapists.

Subjective resistances and counterresistances, while they may be partly aroused by the therapist or patient, always involve transferential, character-ological, and cultural factors. Let us say, for exam-ple, that the therapist comes late to his first session because the subway stalled, and the patient reacts by lambasting the therapist. "You expect me to believe that the subway stalled? Don't make ex-cuses! You came late because you're irresponsi-ble." In this case it is apparent that the patient's response is not a normal or reasonable response, but an overreaction. The patient makes an as-sumption about the therapist's character (he is irresponsible), which implies a transference and also a possible projective identification (the thera-pist represents some disowned attitude in the pa-tient). Hence, his lambasting of the therapist con-stitutes a transference resistance.

The most difficult task for therapists is to distinguish between objective and subjective coun-terresistance. Since there is invariably a resistance to uncovering counterresistances, the tendency is to think that whatever we therapists are thinking, feeling, and doing is objective, which causes us to focus our attention on the patient and away from ourselves. The danger is that of assuming our resistances have been aroused by the patient and have little or nothing to do with our own transfer-ence, character, or cultural biases.

Confucius once said, "I have traveled far and wide and have yet to meet a man who could bring home the judgment against himself." Lao Tzu once said, "To know others is to be knowing; to know yourself is to know all." Shakespeare once said, "To thine own self be true,/And it must follow, as the night the day,/Thou canst not then be false to any man."

## THE RESISTANCE–
## COUNTERRESISTANCE DYAD

Racker (1968) refers to this dyad in speaking about the transference–countertransference relationship. "Just as the transference, according to Freud, is the field in which the principal battles are fought in order to conquer the resistances, so the countertransference is the other half of this field, and on it the principal battles are fought to conquer the analyst's resistances, that is the counterresistances" (p. 19).

The therapy relationship is the only one of its kind. It is the only one in which one person in a two-person relationship is required to have both a personal relationship with a client and to remain objective while doing so. Other professionals, such as physicians or lawyers, are not required to have a personal relationship with their clients—that is, they are not required to deal with personal issues except insofar as they relate to the actual procedures involved. This is what makes psychotherapy unique and also makes it challenging.

When Racker talks about battles, he is not understating the case. Whenever two humans meet, there is always a resistance to getting close.

This may be partly our biological heritage, a natural fear of strangers, an instinct toward territorial aggression. If we sit at a counter in a coffee shop, we try to choose a stool as far away from other humans as possible; when meeting a new person, we have to "break the ice"; when at a cocktail party, we must overcome our fears and "put our best foot forward."

On top of this biological aggression and resistance that is natural to humans and other animal species, there is the resistance that is linked to our interactions with the environment, particularly those in our early childhoods, from which we develop our models for later transferences, our characterological defenses, and our cultural biases. Both the patient and the therapist bring all of these into the therapy office. Both bring genetic and environmental resistances, and from the beginning there is a battle to overcome these resistances. Indeed, there are four battles of resistance going on simultaneously: the patient's battle with self-resistance, the therapist's battle with self-resistance, the patient's battle with the therapist's resistance, and the therapist's battle with the patient's resistance.

The therapist is the chief fighter of this battle. Some patients who are less severely disturbed and have a strong positive transference will help fight this battle. Others, perhaps most, will obstruct and step up the battle—that is, they will resist the overcoming of their resistances. The therapist's job is to battle against both his own and his patient's resistances.

The basic aim of this battle is to bring both

therapist and patient into harmony with themselves and each other. In this sense, psychoanalysis is related to certain Eastern philosophies, such as Taoism (of which I will say more in the next chapter). Harmony, in this sense, means being in the world with the least effort—that is, with the least resistance. It means ridding ourselves of the neurotic, narcissistic, borderline, or psychotic defenses that prevent us from doing so. It means being in the world without denying things we do not want to deal with; without projecting things onto others so that we can quarrel with them, defeat them, and thereby calm our own internal anxiety; without assuaging our guilt through rituals or drugs; without withdrawing from the world and thereby cutting off all possibility for real meaning or gratification; without dominating or submitting or guilt-tripping or somatizing; without doing any of the thousand and one things we do to make being in the world more difficult than it has to be.

As I said, it is the therapist's responsibility to bring about this harmony. To help the patient overcome resistance, Freud (1912) devised the fundamental rule—free association. To help therapists overcome their counterresistance he devised the equivalent of the fundamental rule, *evenly-suspended attention* (1912). Just as we can ascertain the amount of a particular patient's resistance to how well he can free associate, so too a therapist's capacity to *counter-free-associate* is a litmus test of counterresistance. Just as we can say that anything the patient does to obstruct progress is resistance, we can also say that anything the therapist does to obstruct progress is counterresistance.

To repeat what I said earlier, therapists need to focus less on analyzing the patient's resistance and more on analyzing their own. Indeed, whenever therapists become aware of a resistance on the patient's part, they should look for the counterresistance before attempting to interpret the patient's resistance. Often, once the therapist has overcome the counterresistance, the patient's resistance will be easy to resolve. Therapists should not be technicians—machines that analyze and interpret—but participant-observers who model the kind of healthy functioning, sans resistances, that they want the patient to follow.

**2**

---

# To See
# without Seeking

The world's first psychoanalyst was not really Sigmund Freud or even Josef Breuer. It may have been Lao Tzu. And one of his first patients was probably Confucius.

Ssu Ma Ch'ien, who wrote an early history of China, recounts the legendary—some say mythical—meeting between Lao Tzu (which means "the old man") and Confucius some, 2,500 years ago. Confucius was said to be about fifty years younger than Lao Tzu.

On that day, Confucius had come to Lao Tzu for instructions in the rituals of proper conduct. Confucius sat before Lao Tzu—who was the keeper of the Royal Archives and had a reputation of being a wise, although somewhat odd old man—and went on and on about what constituted true virtue, how a man should conduct himself in this situation and that, and referred to the sayings of various authorities on the subject. All at once Lao Tzu stopped him.

"What you are talking about concerns merely the words left by people who have rotted along with their bones. If a man is in tune with the times, he will prosper and go out in a fine carriage; if not, he will drift with the wind. I have heard that the best merchants hide their goods to make themselves appear poor, and that those who have perfected their character pretend to be fools. Get rid of your arrogance, your desires, your ingratiating manners, and your ambitiousness. They are absolutely useless! That's all I have to say to you."

Then, according to the same historian, as Lao Tzu saw Confucius off, he added, "I have heard that rich and superior men give money, while good men give words. I have not been able to win wealth or rank, but I have undeservedly become known as a good man. Anyway, I'll leave you with these words as my parting gift: 'There are men with clever and penetrating minds who are never far from death, since they tend always to criticize others. There are men of wide learning and eloquence who put themselves in danger because they expose the evil deeds of others. Neither a son nor a subject should look upon his person as his own.'"

Confucius left in confusion, and went to his students to exclaim: "I know that birds can fly and fish can swim and beasts can run. I know that there are snares for things that run, nets for those that swim, and arrows for those that fly. But of dragons—I shall never know how they ride the wind and cloud up the sky. Today I saw Lao Tzu, and he is a dragon!"

In essence, Lao Tzu gave Confucius an interpretation and a suggestion he did not want to receive. And his interpretation had to do with the character defenses (i.e., arrogance, manners) of Confucius—his resistances.

Lao Tzu lived at the dawning of a golden age of Chinese thought. This golden age, which came about as a result of the stability of the Chou (Zhou) Dynasty, lasted from about the sixth to the second century B.C. and spawned what came to be known as "the hundred schools." Among the stellar thinkers produced during this era, in addition to Lao Tzu and Confucius, were Mencius (a follower of Confucius), and Chuang Tzu (a follower of Lao Tzu), Yang Chu (noted for his "Epicurean philosophy"), and Mo Tzu (known as a philanthropist). This era was, in some respects, a forerunner of the psychoanalytic movement that sprang up at the end of the nineteenth century, which, in turn, spawned its various schools of psychoanalysis and psychotherapy.

Thus, is was Lao Tzu and other early Taoist philosophers who may have been the first to discover and articulate the concepts of resistance and counterresistance and show how they served as an impediment to living the best of all possible lives. It was they who first observed that less is more. Just as an Olympic swimmer must shed himself of anything extraneous (such as body hair) that might add resistance as he propels himself through the water, so, too, all human beings, according to the Taoists, benefit by shedding extraneous things—physical, characterological, or emotional—that

prevent them from living as effortlessly and naturally as possible, and prevent them from being as
directly in contact with others and with the world
as they could be.

When Lao Tzu tells Confucius that "the best
merchants hide their goods to make themselves
appear poor" and "those who have perfected their
character pretend to be fools," he is alluding to
ridding the self of physical displays of wealth or
grandiosity that might be provocative and therefore become a resistance to harmonious relating.
Similarly, when he tells Confucius to "get rid of
your arrogance, your desires, your ingratiating
manners, and your ambitiousness," he is interpreting his characterological defenses, which become resistances to natural, authentic intimacy
with others and with the world (not to mention
with the self). Before letting Confucius go, he further warns him about "clever and penetrating
minds who are never far from death, since they
tend always to criticize others" and about men of
learning who endanger themselves because "they
expose the evil deeds of others." Here again he is
interpreting some typical characterological defenses—defenses that a psychoanalyst today might
diagnose as narcissistic or paranoid or masochistic.
Unfortunately, Lao Tzu's interpretation was an
ego-dystonic one, which left Confucius enraged
and had him calling Lao Tzu "a dragon!" This
seems to indicate that Lao Tzu had a counterresistance to Confucius that prevented him from giving
an interpretation that Confucius would have been
able to hear. (Perhaps Lao Tzu felt resentful about
the latter's arrogance and grandiosity or was

threatened by it, which compelled him to express himself in this imperious manner.)

The word *Tao*, from which Taoism is derived, is most often translated as the *way*, although it means much more than that. It refers to a path to enlightenment, a way of being in the world, natural harmony, and a kind of childlike innocence. There is an emphasis on stillness, on doing things without ado, on returning to nature's core, and on the obtaining of cosmic consciousness. However, at its essence, the Way means "the path of least resistance."

I have found that looking at resistance from the perspective of Eastern philosophy helps me to see this phenomenon with fresh eyes. The psychoanalytic view of resistance and counterresistance, as recounted in Chapter 1, can not only be confusing, what with all the distinctions and contradictions, but also intellectually distancing. As I pointed out in my opening vignette, psychoanalytic theory can become an ideological resistance against genuine contact with a patient or an intellectual defense against some unconscious perceived threat, such as the threat of being rejected by the transferred father. Taoism brings one back to the earth.

## TAOISM AND PSYCHOANALYSIS

Many have noted a similarity between Eastern paths to enlightenment, as exemplified by Taoism and Zen Buddhism, and Western paths as exemplified by psychoanalysis and other forms of psychotherapy. Among psychoanalysts, Jung (1971) and

Fromm (Fromm, Suzuki, and DeMartino, 1960) have written widely on the subject.

Aside from the concept of resistance and counterresistance, many of the other basic notions of Taoism find parallels in the literature of psychoanalysis and psychotherapy. Lao Tzu notes in various poems of *Tao Te Ching* that "the Way that can be told is not the eternal Way,"* and that "those who Speak do not know; those who know do not speak," and Chuang Tzu asserts that the Way cannot be transmitted to those who are not ready to hear it, for "the wise cannot give the Way to a mind that will not receive it." Similarly, most psychoanalysts believe that whatever change occurs during therapy has to do with the emotional interaction between therapist and patient rather than with words, and they do not give interpretations to patients who are not ready to hear them.

Lao Tzu says, "To be is to do," and urges people to follow the "one true Way . . . to the natural mode," and "return to nature's core." Therapists tell patients to "get in touch with your feelings," and "get centered" and "be yourself." Lao Tzu notes that "to know others is to be knowing; to know yourself is to know all." Freud and other therapists attempt to "make the unconscious conscious" and "expand self-awareness." Lao Tzu speaks of how "the softest and the weakest overcomes the hard and strong," and exhorts people to "know the masculine but show the feminine." Psychoanalysts speak about "adaptability,"

---

*All translations of Lao Tzu and Chuang Tzu are the author's.

"spontaneity," and "getting in touch with your feminine side." Lao Tzu speaks of wise people who can "love without possessing," "do without ado," "guide without intruding," and who are able to "smooth the tangles" and "lose themselves" and rid themselves of "selfish need." Psychoanalysts talk about "healthy ego functioning," "conflict-free functioning," and "resolving complexes," and helping patients transcend their "compulsion to repeat" and work through their "narcissistic grandiosity." Lao Tzu says that the wise "bend with their plights," while fools "insist on their rights." Psychoanalysts are trained to "do whatever will advance therapeutic progress."

Indeed, Lao Tzu himself saw the Way as an antidote to mental sickness:

> To know that you do not know
> Is to be sane.
> To not know and think you know
> Is to be sick
>
> To be sick of being sick
> Is to stop being sick.
> To stay sick of being sick
> Is to stay sane.
> —Lao-Tzu tzu, poem 71

The process of gaining enlightment is also similar to that of becoming analyzed. The ancient Tao masters as well as modern Zen masters take on followers and work with them in one-to-one relationships, as do psychoanalysts and psychotherapists. Lao Tzu speaks of stillness and of how

important it is to "do without doing," and Seng
Ts'an says, "To follow nature is to wander freely;
fettered thoughts are frightened of what's true."
Similarly, Freud invented the term "free association," urging patients to verbalize their thoughts as
they came up without trying to think of anything in
particular, recognizing that people tend to censor
all that they normally say and thereby avoid the
truth. Lao Tzu says, "If you do not vie with life, life
will not vie with you," while Freud focused on the
destructiveness of a patient's resistance to the
therapy process, seeing it as analogous to resistance to intimacy and life itself. Lao Tzu tells people
to become "an uncarved block of wood" and to
return "to childhood once more." Psychoanalysts
help patients regress to early childhood so that
they can work through fixations and regain a less
corrupted (by psychopathology) way of being.

Taoism and Zen aim toward enlightenment
resulting from "inner peace" and oneness with the
world. Psychoanalysis aims toward awareness resulting from integration of "disowned parts of the
self" and "adjustment" to the world. The enlight-
ened Taoist master sees the oneness and relativity
of things; as Seng Ts'an puts it, "Wisdom holds no
right and finds no wrong." The psychoanalyst is
trained to be neutral and have no biases or preconceptions or any private ends in working with a
patient. Lao Tzu exhorts people to "tone down the
brightness," "stay behind." Chuang Tzu, elabo-
rating on this theme, describes a man who studied
with a master in order to eliminate anything from
his personality that might make him stand out; the
result was that people did not to know what to

make of him and hence began to admire him. Psychoanalysts are trained to maintain a "blank screen," to not reveal anything about themselves to the patient so that the patient will not know what to make of them and hence be able to admire or scorn them, that is, to project and study what they project onto the psychoanalyst. Lao Tzu speaks of an "egoless state," and says that the wise "have no needs of their own" and can therefore "know the needs of others." Psychoanalysts talk about the importance for analysts to work through their narcissistic needs so that they can be truly empathic toward patients. Lao Tzu even refers to the collective unconscious (this is my interpretation, of course; he calls it the spirits of ancestors) advising leaders to rule with concern in order to keep "the fires of the collective unconscious [spirits of ancestors] from burning up people." Psychoanalysts speak not only of the collective unconscious, but of the individual unconscious (composed of buried memories and feelings from the past, including those of ancestors passed on from generation to generation and embedded in emotionally contagious behavioral patterns). Psychoanalysts also study the effect of the unconcious on an individual's present life.

As a psychoanalyst, I can testify that as the result of my training, I have had to change drastically the way I relate not only to patients, but to everybody. Through long years of training analysis, as well as years of supervision, I have had to get in touch with my unconscious feelings and thoughts. If there is any aspect of my behavior or manner of which I am not aware or in control, my patients will jump on it; if I have too much brightness (pride), they will fix on it and attack it; if I am prone to getting involved in certain kinds of entanglements in my life and have not resolved them, those same entanglements will occur in my therapy relationships and impede progress; if I want to help my patients (rather than being abstinent), I will give them something to defeat or put pressure on them; if I have not resolved my own needs for love or approval, I will not be able to empathize completely with them and will be vulnerable to their rejections; if I have any kind of religious, political, racial, or philosophical bias through which I view the patient, no genuine progress will be made. Therefore, I have found that Lao Tzu's *Tao Te Ching*, with its succinct and beautiful sayings with regard to these matters, is virtually a training manual for the practice of psychoanalysis and psychotherapy.

Chuang Tzu provides an excellent example of how Lao Tzu "worked," therapeutically, with a disturbed man named Ki. This story illustrates how Lao Tzu used neutrality, the blank screen, and confrontation, although he did not know it as such. Ki walked for one hundred days to meet Lao Tzu because he had heard that he was a wise man. Upon meeting him, he found out some facts about him that made him feel disappointed in him. (Lao Tzu had recently sent away his younger sister, supposedly because she was feeding his rice to rats.) Therefore he told Lao Tzu, "Now that I'm here, I see that you are not a wise man at all" (a variation of devaluing the therapist, which might be seen as a character trait of a borderline personality.) Lao Tzu did not seem concerned, and he did not give any reply. The next day Ki returned and confessed to Lao Tzu that he had taunted him the day before. He said that his mood was better this day, although, "I do not understand why." The story then continues (Chuang Tzu, Ch. XIII:8):

> Lao Tzu said, "It appears I have freed myself from the bondage of sagehood—of being knowing, spiritual, and good. Yesterday you could have called me an ox or a horse if you liked. If one man gives vent to a feeling and another man does not accept it, the first man will suffer all the more. I did not behave any differently yesterday than usual; I do not change for the occasion."

Ki then asked Lao Tzu how he could improve himself, and Lao Tzu told him he was repulsive, pretentious, anxious, cunning, and insincere, and pointed out that if he ever tried to leave town, his personality was such that he would probably be arrested as a thief.

What happened in this story? On the first day, Lao Tzu allowed Ki to taunt him without showing any concern or making any reply. He remained neutral—did not offer any judgment about what Ki told him—and became a blank screen, showing no concern. Ki, like today's therapy patient, then seemed to develop a negative transference: He made assumptions about the kind of person Lao Tzu was by transfering onto him attributes that probably belonged to a primary figure in his life, such as his own father, who was perhaps punitive and harsh. (Let us further speculate that Ki's father rejected him the way Lao Tzu apparently rejected his younger sister.) There may also have been other factors involved in this initial reactions; borderline patients, for example, tend to use the defense mechanism of splitting (dissociating themselves from their own negative thoughts and feelings and projecting them onto others).

However, on the second day the negative transference or projection had become resolved, and Ki saw Lao Tzu again with admiration. Lao Tzu understood that his response to Ki had had a transforming effect and explained that he had been able to be neutral—that he was freed of his bondage to the image of a sage and had no narcissistic stake in being seen as wise, so Ki's remarks did not upset him. Moreover, he knew that had he not allowed Ki to give vent to his feelings, those feelings would have become stronger; therefore he accepted them. By being neutral and blank and not resisting Ki's projections and feelings, the ideas and feelings went away on their own, and Ki was able to listen to Lao Tzu's frank critical assessment of his personality.

This story, whether true or not, shows that Chuang Tzu knew something about the process of therapy, and about counterresistance. Lao Tzu did not offer any resistance to Ki's projections or devaluation, and withheld any interpretation until the next day, when he knew Ki would be able to hear it. He was in perfect harmony with the situation, and therefore did nothing to obstruct progress.

## RESOLVING COUNTERRESISTANCE BY
## DOING NOTHING

In poem 47, Lao Tzu states one of the main themes of his philosophy, which bears directly upon the subject of counterresistance and psychotherapy:

> Would you run outside
> To study the earth?
> Would you throw your windows wide
> To study its birth?
>
> The further you go,
> The less you will know.
>
> Know without going.
> See without seeking.
> Do without doing.

In psychotherapy, too, the less one does the better it is. Perhaps the hardest thing for a novice therapist to learn is not to try to cure a patient. The curing takes place of its own accord. The desire to cure a patient—or to do anything to or for a patient—is a counterresistance. It is a resistance to allowing the process to unfold at its own pace. Perhaps the second hardest thing for a novice to learn is not to try to understand the patient, but rather to "see without seeking." The understanding will come in and of itself, and the more patients can find out for themselves without the therapist telling them, the better it is for them. The more a therapist tries to be a therapist ("The further you go . . ."), the less the therapist will be a therapist ("the less you will know"). Again, in Poem 57, Lao Tzu writes:

> If I do nothing
> People will reform themselves.
> If I fight nothing
> People will settle themselves.
> If I push nothing
> People will advance themselves.
> If I crave nothing
> People will accept themselves.

The theme of taking the path of least resistance reappears in many variations throughout Lao Tzu's poems. He speaks of doing nothing, of being still, of being humble, of being a valley for the world, of being like an infant, of being soft, of being feminine, of yielding, of staying behind, and of being formless. One of the most succinct expressions of this theme, however, appears in Poem 68, in which he uses the metaphor of the solider:

> Great soldiers do not grunt.
> Great fighters do not grind.
> Great victors do not vie.
> Great leaders stay behind.
>
> This is the art of yielding.
> This is the art of joining.
> This is ancient unity.
> This is natural harmony.

Lao Tzu believed that there was a universal path that any human had to travel in order to become a healthy, contented, actualized human being. All philosophies, therapies, and religions have struggled to find that path, some more successfully than others. Lao Tzu happens to have been one of the most articulate in describing that path in metaphorical terms, while Freud described it in the language of nineteenth century metapsychology. Counterresistance by any other name will still be counterresistance.

To accept life without wanting to change it; to study the natural order of things and work within that order and not against it; to be at one with nature, with the understanding that nature provides for one and all without picking and choosing; to view the world through nature's eyes, without human judgments, the search for right and wrong, and the collecting of injustices or pointing of fingers; to be humble as a child in order to "stand under" and "understand" life—this is what Lao Tzu taught.

Some have misinterpreted Taoism as advocating a form of self-denial and loss of real contact with the world; indeed, some mental health professionals have painted it as a kind of schizoid phenomenon. Nothing could be more from the truth, although people with schizoid personalities are attracted to and misuse and misinterpret it that way. Once, when one of his students asked him to clarify what he meant when he said that wise people are without passion and desire, Chuang Tzu replied that the wise do not "do any inward harm" to their body through their "likings and dislikings; they always "live effortlessly" and do not "crave life or press for more." The paradox that he wanted to convey is that only when one is able to be completely humble and have no neurotic or narcissistic self-interest can one be completely actualized and one's life be fully and perfectly in tune with nature. Only when we know and master our tendencies to resist can we be completely free to participate totally and healthily in life (Poem 56):

> And thus wisely be
> Above joy or pain
> Beyond praise and curse
> Ahead of loss or gain
> At the top of the universe.

# 3

# Common "Symptoms" of Counterresistance

Before getting into a fuller discussion of the three main types of counterresistance, I would like to describe some general "symptoms" of counterresistance. I use the word *symptom* because the examples of counterresistance under consideration are really surface expressions of a complex, largely unconscious process involving the acting out of ego-dystonic memories, thoughts, and impulses.

The list in Table 3–1 is not exhaustive. Symptoms of counterresistance are infinite, as infinite as any list of symptoms of resistance would be. However, this list will serve to indicate the types of behaviors that would be symptomatic of counterresistance and would therefore obstruct therapeutic progress. Most of the items on the list are self-explanatory, but a few may need further elaboration.

## Table 3-1. Examples of Counterresistance

Coming late for sessions.
Forgetting sessions.
Canceling sessions.
Falling asleep during sessions.
Clearing the throat during sessions.
Thinking of a patient between sessions.
Avoiding eye contact with patient.
Making too much eye contact with patient.
Forgetting a patient's name.
Saying a patient's name too much.
Talking too little or too much.
Smiling too little or too much.
Charging too little or too much.
Denying feelings.
Expressing feelings impulsively.
Avoiding a certain subject.
Overconcern with a certain subject.
Appeasing the patient.
Defying the patient.
Avoiding confrontation.
Confronting with a vengeance.
Flirting with a patient.
Angrily rebuffing a patient's flirtation.
Apologizing to a patient before patient has expressed feelings.
Refusing ever to apologize.
Forcing patient to stick to the point.
Helping patient to ramble.
Impatience with a patient.
Boredom with a patient.
Fascination with a patient.
A desire to cure a patient.
A desire to understand a patient.
A desire to dominate or submit to a patient.
A desire to entertain or be entertained by a patient.
A desire to tease or be teased by a patient.
A desire to admire or be admired by a patient.
A desire to make up for the patient's past misery.
Giving instructions that can't be followed.
Giving orders that arouse defiance.
Giving unwanted advice.
Putting patients into a double bind.
Giving mixed (verbal and nonverbal) signals.
Responding in a hostile tone to a patient's hostility.
Sticking to one technique or school of therapy.
Inability to understand something the patient keeps repeating.
Ending the therapy too soon.
Holding on to the patient.
Beating the patient.
Raping the patient.
Killing the patient.

In general, a therapist needs to avoid extremes. Open-mindedness, flexibility, and steering a middle course generally constitute the best policy. "Neither a borrower nor a lender be," Shakespeare said, "for loan oft loses both itself and friend, and borrowing dulls the edge of husbandry." This epitomizes the principle of the middle course. The therapist should, in general, not exploit or be exploited by, feed or be fed by, ride or be ridden by the patient, emotionally, intellectually, or monetarily. He should follow Lao Tzu's path of least resistance. Most of the items on the list concern a therapist's saying or doing too little or too much, and thereby going to one extreme or another.

For example, some therapists, particularly certain classical psychoanalysts, will refuse to ever apologize for anything. They have been taught that an apology, no matter what the circumstances, gives the patient a message that the therapist needs approval, wants to be liked, or can be manipulated. However, there are some circumstances when an apology is warranted and helpful, and not to give one will be a counterresistance. If the therapist comes late once, no apology is necessary. If it happens repeatedly and the patient becomes understandably disturbed (and is given the chance to ventilate feelings about it), an apology may not only be necessary but vital, demonstrating that the therapist respects the patient enough to show consideration, thereby preventing a widening breach. In some cases the apology might be accompanied by a discussion of "What's going on between us now?" in which the therapist takes responsibility for his counterresistance and encourages the patient to do the same about any possible resistance. Again, the therapist should avoid extremes, such as giving the apology either too fliply or too abjectly.

To apologize or not to apologize depends on the patient. There was an instance in my own practice in which I kept double-scheduling the same patient. She was a borderline patient who was calling nearly every week to change her appointment. I had more resentment about her constant changing of appointments than I realized, and this resentment got acted out by my scheduling her at the same time as another patient on two or three occasions. When she came late for her rescheduled appointment and discovered that I had another patient inside my office, she would be furious. Because she was a tyrannical, paranoid person who was constantly threatening to quit unless she got her way, I did not apologize to her, for to do so would have been tantamount to giving in to a threat. However, I did apologize to another patient at around that same time after I kept oversleeping and coming late for his 8:30 A.M. appointment. This patient was a passive young man whose parents made him their scapegoat, and who had therefore been trained to assume that everything bad that happened to him was his fault. For him, my taking responsibility for my counterresistance was a corrective emotional experience.

Another subtle counterresistance is the desire to understand a patient. On the surface, this seems laudable. Should not a therapist try to understand a patient? But if by understanding a patient we mean that a therapist is impatient to understand or bothered if he does not understand something or everything about a patient, or if he has a need to explain his understanding to the patient and not allow the patient to come to that understanding in his own way in his own time, this would be symptomatic of counterresistance. In my early days of doing therapy I often felt lost if I did not immediately understand patients and know what to do about them, and I tended to be in a hurry to convey my understanding to them. When I felt lost, I would either lapse into silence or ask too many questions (trying to get at the elusive understanding). Either way, my patients did not sense that I was in tune with them and therapeutic progress was hampered.

What I discovered is that in many, if not most, cases it does not matter whether I immediately understand everything about my patients. What matters is that I set up an environment in which they and I can find out what is inside of them and in which neither they nor I resist or counterresist these encounters. Understanding will come when it comes, and interpretations can be given when they can be given.

Other subtle instances of counterresistance have to do with the double messages we give patients. A therapist may schedule an appointment with a patient in such a way that the patient does not understand clearly and will therefore miss the appointment. This is caused by a counterresistance in the therapist that causes him to, let us say, mumble the time or date of the appointment or in some other way convey to the patient that he is ambivalent about it. On an unconscious level, the therapist may want the patient to miss the appointment in order to have an excuse to act out some countertransference feeling. If the patient does miss the appointment, the therapist will then analyze the patient's resistance without ever having become aware of his own counterresistance, and since it was expressed in such a subtle way, the patient may not understand it either.

Therapists can often put patients into a double bind without knowing it. For example, a therapist may greet the patient coldly each session and then remark,"You never smile when you enter the room." The therapist is giving a mixed message; nonverbally he is cold, rejecting, verbally he is rebuking the patient for being cold and rejecting. This puts the patient in a double bind. If he smiles, the therapist will reject him with a cold look, but if he doesn't smile, the therapist will rebuke him. Whenever patients are put into a double bind, it stirs resentment, disturbs the relationship between therapist and patient, and impedes progress. It can also ignite a negative transference, since it will be a reminder of parents, who are prone to putting children into double-bind situations in order to manipulate and control them. ("You're acting just like your father," a mother may say to her son when he is shouting at her. He is then forced to stop shouting and suppress his feelings or be shamed for expressing them.

Another subtle form of counterresistance has to do with giving mixed signals. A patient may be hysterically flirtatious, talking obsessively about erotic impulses toward the therapist and insistently asking personal questions. The therapist responds in one way verbally and in another way nonverbally. Verbally, he tells the patient that while he and she, for obvious reasons, cannot act out their erotic impulses, she needs to feel free to explore them therapeutically. Nonverbally, he may blush or sit with his arms and legs folded or smile too much or lapse into silences, indicating that he is indeed affected by her feelings and uncomfortable with them. This double message will be both confusing to the patient and provocative; hence, it will impede therapeutic progress and keep the relationship stuck in the flirtatious mode.

This brings me to another common symptom of counterresistance, that of a therapist feeling uncomfortable with feelings that are being aroused by a patient. Usually the feelings that make a therapist most uncomfortable are sexual or aggressive. Denying them only makes matters worse. If patients sense that a therapist is uncomfortable with sexual or aggressive feelings, they either become discouraged from expressing them or encouraged to express them even more, depending on whether they have a positive or negative transference. It is better for therapists to admit to patients that they are feeling uncomfortable with a particular feeling than to deny it. "I'm feeling a little uncomfortable about your sexual thoughts about me," the therapist may say, "but I can deal with it. Please go on." The patient, knowing that the therapist is aware of his or her counterresistance, will be less encouraged either to back off or persist. And should the patient take such an admission as an opportunity to analyze the therapist and ask why he is feeling uncomfortable, the therapist can reply, "I'm not sure. Why do you think I'm feeling uncomfortable?" This puts the onus back onto the patient and makes it clear that the therapist does not need an analyst.

Adhering rigidly to one technique is another of the most common symptoms of counterresistance, and one that is commonly ignored. Since nearly all institutes of psychotherapy adhere to one school or another, their candidates are trained to follow one technique or set of techniques, while despising others. A therapist trained in the techniques of self psychology might be reluctant to interpret or confront a patient, such as a borderline patient, who clearly requires an interpretation or a confrontation. The therapist may justify this reluctance under the rubric of self psychology, quoting Kohut or some other authority to back it up. (For more on this subject, see Chapter 7.)

Many beginning therapists misunderstand the concept of empathy. They think that it means showing the patient that they care, when it actually means being able to put themselves in the patient's shoes. They inevitably equate displays of caring and affection with empathy, but such displays are usually related to a need to be liked and to be seen as good and loving, while true empathy means being in tune with patients' needs, whether their need is to be loved or yelled at by the therapist.

One of my first patients came to me with a tale about childhood abuse. She was a pretty young woman who wore her hair in a braid that curled around her thin long neck and dangled on her chest. As she spoke to me in a scarcely audible whisper about the retarded older brother who would sock her in the eyes and kick her in the shins—and about the parents who always took the side of the brother—she would tug on the braid, gazing sadly off into the murky New York sky that blinked through the half-closed blinds on my window. Sometimes she would put the end of the braid in her mouth and suck on it, and sometimes she would twirl it around her fingers. I found that braid hypnotic, and would watch her playing with it and listen to her tale of woe and feel tears in my eyes.

In those days I sat facing my clients. As I sat facing her, feeling the tears sliding down my cheek, I thought, "Now she'll see my tears and know that I really care about her. When she sees this, all the pent-up hurt and longing inside of her will gush out, and she will cry out in pain and joy and tell me how grateful she is that she has finally found a man who is sensitive enough and nice enough to really care as nobody has cared before." This did not happen. Instead, several weeks went by, with more tales of abuse and more braid twirling and sucking and more tears dripping from my eyes. Finally, one day she looked up at me as though seeing me for the first time. "This is it," I thought, "the moment of truth."

She leaned toward me. "There's something I must tell you."

I looked back at her, the tears hanging bravely from my cheeks, and smiled lovingly. "Yes?"

"I hate tears. I think it's disgusting when a man cries. It makes me want to puke."

"I see." I felt my smile trying to become a grimace, but through the use of a Zen relaxation technique I quickly caught myself and kept my smile intact. "What is it about a man crying that turns you off?" I asked

"I'm not sure. I think it has to do with my brother."

"What about him?"

"He was always crying, and my parents would fall for it every time. He was disgusting, actually. I'd look up at him and he'd be all puffy and have these big crocodile tears all over his face."

"It must have been awful."

"It was."

She stared at my cheeks with disdain, and I had a great urge to quickly wipe the tears away, but at the same time I did not want to call any more attention to them. So I smiled back at her, as my cheeks began to itch. Somehow I managed to finish the session. She called later that week to say she did not have the money to continue. Tears, I realized are not necessarily perceived by patients as gifts from a fairy godfather, but more often as a demand for love or gratitude or sympathy. I gave her what I thought was a display of empathy, but in actuality it was a display of need and a counterresistance: I was counterresistant to hearing about her brother's abuse, for it aroused guilt in me stemming from my own childhood sibling rivalry.

I made somewhat the same mistake with another borderline patient who needed a confrontation and told me so. She came to me saying that she had dumped her last therapist, who did not understand her and kept wanting her to talk about her past, when what she really wanted was help in solving practical problems in the present. I said I would help her to do that and we spent two sessions discussing, in a very practical way, her immediate career and education problems. The following week she called and said she was quitting, that I was not helping her at all. I asked her to come in, and during the course of our discussion she said, almost as an aside, that she thought she needed me to be harder on her in order to get her going. What she meant by being harder on her, I now realize, is that she needed me to confront her.

She stayed for another session, during which she resisted further discussion of her sudden desire to quit, and I joined that resistance by again focusing on her career and education issues. She had decided that she wanted to go to London to study, and I gave her information about moderately priced hotels I had stayed in and advised her on where to find the cheapest airline rates. At the end of the session she left, beaming as though she had never been helped so much in her life. The next week she came in, slapped her check into my hands, and said, "I'm not staying."

"You've paid for the session," I hastily remarked, "so you might as well use it."

"I don't want to use it!" She glared at me as if she suspected me of murdering, maiming, and raping everybody in her family in some past life. "I'm leaving now!"

"This is kind of sudden."

"That's right, it is.

"Did I do something wrong?"

"I don't want to talk about it. It's not working, that's all," she said, spitting the words at me, and she walked out in a huff.

She was in a rage because, in effect, I had let her down. I had not taken her clue; I had not "been hard on her" and confronted her. Instead, I had thrown myself with renewed zeal into the process of helping her solve her problems. This had obviously not worked the first time, yet I had done it again. She saw through my cowardly nice-guy pose and had contempt for me.

Afterward (hindsight is wonderful for both therapists and writers) I realized that my counterresistance had manifested itself in this reluctance to confront her. I was fooled by her apparent positive response to my problem-solving approach and lulled into thinking that she needed an empathic and supportive environment. In reality I wanted to avoid dealing with her rage, which I sensed might be volatile and require me to get into the trenches with her. So I had ignored her clue and lost the patient.

I have since learned that many borderlines and psychotics do not respond to a warm, empathic environment, but instead crave a confrontation that will serve to meet their force with force, show that the therapist is in touch with and can handle his own and the patient's aggression, stablize the patient, and prevent the buildup of a hostile environment from which the patient will have to flee. It also makes the patient feel understood and allows the therapist to constructively express, rather than stuff, his countertransference feelings. There are simply times a therapist must meet subjective hate with objective hate, and to avoid doing so is a counterresistance. It may be one of the most prevalent counterresistances of all.

It is important for therapists to look for and recognize these and the multitude of other symptoms of counterresistance. This is the first step toward resolving their resistances to patients before they get out of hand and cause problems. If a therapist ignores the subtle symptoms, they will develop into less subtle and more complex symptoms. Little symptoms soon become big symptoms that will become increasingly more difficult to resolve and reverse.

If a therapist finds himself strangling a patient, for example, that is usually a sign that many subtler symptoms of counterresistance have been previously ignored.

# 4

# Countertransference
# Resistance

As I previously mentioned, Gill (1982), while making a distinction between characterological defenses and interpersonal resistance, nevertheless stated that "resistance can be expressed only in the transference." Upon closer inspection, the meaning of this statement is rather vague. Does he mean that all resistance *is* transference? Or does he mean that all resistance—no matter whether its source is early childhood trauma, outside social forces, or characterological defensiveness—must be expressed in the transference since, according to many psychoanalysts, particularly Kleinians, everything said by the patient and therapist in therapy is transference and countertransference?

I am making a distinction between counter-transference resistance and characterological resistance, even though both forms of resistance are

expressed in the transference and both are generally outcomes of early childhood development. The
distinction has to do with the fact that countertransference resistance arises specifically in relation to a particular patient and to the kind of
resistance that patient brings to the therapy relationship. Characterological counterresistance, on
the other hand, has little or nothing to do with the
patient's type of resistance, but is the characteristic way the therapist resists in all aspects of life,
in and out of the therapy office, and is an expression of his characterological defenses. I am making
a further distinction between these two types of
counterresistance and cultural counterresistance,
which is not an expression of transference at all,
but a displacement and projection of social pressures and values onto the patient.

Not only are the definitions of transference and
resistance—as well as those of countertransference
and counterresistance—unclear in psychoanalytic
literature, but there is also a debate about whether
everything that occurs in the therapy relationship
*is* transference, or whether there is a nontransference, real relationship as well. Greenson (1967) is
among those who argue for a real relationship.
While Freud attributed the working alliance between therapist and patient to a positive transference, Greenson disagreed, asserting that the core
of the working alliance is to be found in the real or
nontransference relationship between the therapist and patient.

Looking at this from the perspective of the
therapist, I believe that there is a real relationship
between the therapist and patient, and one of the

therapist's jobs is not only to interpret the transference and countertransference resistance, but also
to contrast it with the real relationship. If a patient
fears being entrapped by a therapist when, in fact,
the therapist has never given any indication of
such desires, this is transference. If, on the other
hand, a patient fears being entrapped by a therapist who stares menacingly at the patient, this is at
least in part a real relationship. If a therapist craves
being with a particular patient because that patient
satisfies some narcissistic need for admiration, that
is countertransference. If a therapist enjoys a particular patient because they share many mutual
interests and are alike and in agreement in many
ways, this may be a real, healthy human bonding.

It is the therapist's capacity to have a real
relationship with the patient—and contrast it with
the distortions that accrue from the influx of transferential, characterological, and cultural factors—
that is of crucial importance. When therapists are
beset with countertransference impulses and are
resisting and obstructing the therapy process
themselves, they cannot perform this basic task.

Countertransference resistance is perhaps the
most common way in which therapists obstruct
therapeutic progress. Something about the patient
provokes a counterresistance because it arouses
unresolved feelings from the therapist's past. One
way this can occur is when the therapist has a
complementary identification with the patient and
hence, unconsciously, joins the patient's resistance. A patient may constantly talk in a discon-
nected monotone and avoid dealing with important
issues, which arouses in the therapist a feeling of

boredom and sleepiness. The therapist may know
that the patient is resisting, but, through identification with him, joins that resistance (counterresists) in order to spare the patient's feelings. Because both the patient and the therapist had harsh,
critical parents, a collusion of overprotectiveness
becomes resistance and counterresistance; the patient continues to talk in a monotone, the therapist
falls asleep, and progress is stalled.

Or, a patient may be constantly and relentlessly critical of the therapist and the therapist
begins to criticize the patient in return, through
hostile interpretations delivered in an angry tone.
The therapist's inability to tolerate the angry feelings provoked by the patient's criticism and to
respond constructively (expressing his anger in an
objective manner) is another instance of countertransference resistance. This therapist, as in the
previous case, had critical parents, and the patient's criticisms aroused memories of being criti-
cized in the past. He is unable to objectify and
control his countertransference feelings, so he impulsively acts them out. If he had been able to
objectify them, he might have used them to understand the patient and given the patient a similar
interpretation without a hostile intent; he would
have expressed an objective counterresistance to
the patient's criticism and met force with force,
with the aim of achieving insight and closeness.
Whenever a therapist has a hostile intent—a desire
to harm the patient—that is a sign of a subjective
counterresistance, or in this case a subjective countertransference resistance.

Generally countertransference resistance is

provoked when some aspect of the patient's personality or behavior is reminiscent of a primary figure in the therapist's past. The patient's personality or behavior sets off in the therapist a regression back to a fixation point or points, rekindling memories and feelings and reanimating complexes that arose during this phase. Thereafter, the therapist forms a transference to the patient, displacing onto the patient patterns of feelings and behavior that he originally experienced toward a primary figure. This is not one of the therapist's characteristic ways of responding, not a character defense, but more of an isolated response to this particular situation, the chief function of which is to protect him against the possible reemergence of traumatic memories, anxieties, and impulses from early childhood, as well as to protect the primary figures (his parents, siblings) in that original situation by maintaining the original repression. The secondary gain of countertransference resistance is to control or defeat the surrogate (in this case, the patient) and maintain a semblence of homeostasis. (See Table 4–1).

Sometimes a therapist's resistance may be a combination of countertransference and characterological factors, as I pointed out in the first chapter. In other cases it will be clear that it is one or the other. It is helpful for the therapist to know whether it is countertransference resistance or characterological counterresistance. If it is the former, the therapist must study the patient's personality and behavior to determine what set it off. If it is the latter, it will have little or nothing to do with the patient, and the therapist will have to take full

**Table 4–1.** Three Types of Counterresistance

| | Origin | Main Defensive Mode | Primary Frunction | Secondary Function | Secondary Gain |
|---|---|---|---|---|---|
| *Countertransference Resistance* | Early childhood trauma | Transference and Displacement | Defend against reemergence of traumatic situation, usually in early childhood | Protection of primary figures | Control or defeat of surrogates; maintenance of homeostasis |
| *Characterological Counterresistance* | Early childhood trauma | Transference, Displacement, and Repetition Compulsion | Defend against perceived threats to the self: reengulfment, degradation, eruption of murderous/ suicidal feelings | Protection of primary figures | Control or defeat of surrogates; reversal of traumatic relationship |
| *Cultural Counterresistance* | Cultural forces | Displacement and Projection | Defend against perceived threat to one's group, social stigma, guilt, feelings of inferiority | Protection of "group" | Control or defeat of "enemy"; maintenance of territory |

responsibility for the counterresistance and resistance it invokes and study his own characterological tendencies.

## HAROLD SEARLES AND SYMBIOTIC CLINGING

Harold Searles (1979) studied a kind of countertransference resistance that occurs when therapists work with schizophrenic patients. He traced it to a fixation in the symbiotic phase, stating that "psychotherapy with the schizophrenic patient tends to involve the therapist's feelings at the level of his own early childhood experiences" (p. 524). During the early part of the therapy, the therapist and patient become enmeshed in a symbiotic relationship that is a re-creation of the one to which the patient is fixated—the infantile relationship with the mother. This relationship is both gratifying and hazardous.

According to Searles, individuals develop fixations in this symbiotic phase when the normal mother–infant symbiosis fails to resolve into the individuation of mother and child, due to deep ambivalence on the part of the mother that hinders the integration and differentiation of the infant's and toddler's ego. The child's failure to individuate results in fragmentation (splitting) of the ego, and the core of the personality remains unformed. In therapy, the patient regresses back to the this early level of ego development, the level at which the infant is merged with the mother and cannot yet distinguish clearly between itself and the mother and between inner and outer worlds.

The therapist will experience a corresponding regression, feeling alternately maternal and infantile with respect to the patient; indeed, there will be in the therapist a corresponding loss of the ability to distinguish between therapist and patient. At the same time, the therapist will experience intense feelings of grandiosity, the feeling "of being a God, the Creator in the therapeutic situation, of being the only conceivable Pygmalion for this Galatea" (Searles 1979, p. 546). It is an extraordinarily intense experience, akin to the kind of experience a mother has while nursing an infant, and the therapist is prone to the same intoxication with omnipotence as is a mother.

However, when a patient progresses to what Searles calls the "phase of resolution" from the symbiosis, when the patient begins to reach out to others and individuate from the therapist, the therapist is smitten by countertransference resistance. "The therapist feels a clear realization that he himself is no longer indispensable to the patient; he realizes, that is, that he himself is not the only conceivable therapist who can help the patient complete the journey to health" (p. 546). The therapist who has not resolved his own symbiotic fixations may at this point tend to cling to the patient and even to behave in such a way as to drive the patient back into a symbiosis. (that is, to repeat what the mother did in the first place).

He recounts how a hebephrenic patient with whom he had worked for a number of years began to gradually come out of the symbiosis and to radiate "with disconcerting suddenness" a self-containment that should have been a welcome improvement. Now, instead of expecting Searles to be everything and everybody for her she spent the hours of her sessions saying very little and looking "calmly, appraisingly, and objectively" at Searles. Although she was not actively rejecting as she had been earlier, during the ambivalent phase, Searles felt rejected and resented this individuation. He had impulses of clinging to her, and of behaving in such a way as to knock down her newly felt confidence. Fortunately he was able to objectify these countertransference feelings and the impulse to resist and did not act them out.

At this phase, Searles adds, some patients will test the therapist by threatening to change therapists. By presenting the therapist with this threat of separation, the patient wants to find out if the latter can face it squarely without resorting to trying to reestablish the mother–infant symbiosis. One of Searles's patients, with whom he had worked for seven years, asked to use his telephone so that she could call the Director of Psychotherapy and ask for a change of therapists. Searles had the impulse to resist this request. But he again objectified his feelings, overcame this impulse, and allowed her to make the call. "In retrospect," he notes, " I have seen this as a crucial experience for her, that I freely allowed her to do this although her changing therapists would have meant a great personal loss to me, and although I felt it quite possible that she might succeed in that endeavor" (p. 550).

In cases of this type, the countertransference feelings are aroused by a specific symbiotic transference, which draws the therapist into a similar countertransference. If the therapist has an unresolved fixation of his own in the symbiotic stage, he would be prone to countertransference resistance. His own resistance would involve a transference of a pattern and quality of relating associated with that stage onto the patient, as well as a displacement of intense infantile-erotic feelings. There would be a defense, particularly in the phase of resolution, against the separation-anxiety feelings that the therapist originally experienced with respect to his own mother and then repressed, as well as a resistance to recalling the feelings of intense rage at the mother. By the therapist's clinging to this symbiotic relationship, there would be a secondary gain of controlling the patient and keeping her in that stage so that he might remain as the powerful mother figure and maintain a semblance of homeostasis. This is one of the primary hazards for therapists working with schizophrenics.

## THE GUILTY THERAPIST
## AND THE BATTERED PATIENT

One of the most difficult patients for a therapist to handle is a battered woman. Such women are difficult for any therapist because they are constantly complaining about being battered and abused by their boyfriend or spouse and are generally unable to do anything about it or to leave the situation. This arouses feelings of rage, exasperation, and hopelessness in the therapist—the very feelings that the patient denies.

One such patient, a young woman nearing 30,

entered treatment with a youngish male therapist under my supervision. From the beginning she complained of having her jaw broken, teeth knocked out, bruised arms and legs, cigarettes being stubbed out on her arms, and a multitude of mental tortures. Within six months the therapist was full of guilt toward the woman and anger at her husband. He had fantasies of going to the apartment and telling the husband off, rescuing the patient, marrying the patient and treating her well, and of traveling with her to Bermuda.

Increasingly he found the he could not tolerate her diatribes about her husband. After a few minutes, he would stop her and ask her why she was staying with him. He tried vainly to get her to analyze the situation. He pushed her toward taking practical measures to leave. He lectured her about the harm that was being done to her body and mind. She would seem to listen to him and would promise to make arrangements to leave, but it was all simply to appease him.

This patient, like most battered women, had an extremely weak and dependent ego. She had been orphaned by her mother at an early age and had suffered various kinds of abuse as a child, both sexual and physical, from a stepfather and from institutions. She was terrified of leaving her spouse because it would replicate the loss of her mother; she would gladly suffer just about any kind of abuse from her husband to stay with him and experience his approval.

The patient's transference toward the therapist alternated from viewing him as an extremely idealistic mother who would save her (which she dreamed about so often when she was in orphan-

ages) to seeing him as a threatening, lustful stepfather who might molest or abuse her. Each of these
transferences came with displacements of wishes
and feelings. The former included the wish, even
the expectation, that the therapist would save her;
the latter included all the rage at her stepfather, as
well as the rage at her mother, which she had split
off and directed at her stepfather. Each transference
entailed a particular kind of resistance to the therapy. In the former, the patient's idealistic image of
and magical expectations from the therapist ob-
structed progress, hampering the therapist's efforts
to relate to her in a real way about the situation. If
he could not rescue her magically (take her away
with him, etc.), she was disappointed and bitter and
had no use for him. Hence, she was wary and angry
at him and kept him at a distance, refusing to talk
about dreams or the details of her relationship with
her spouse or of her early childhood for fear that the
therapist might become aroused by and take ad-
vantage of these revelations.

These particular resistances by the patient
aroused in the therapist a countertransference resistance that also oscillated. When she was in the
mother transference, he had impulses to rescue her
and take her away with him. When she was in the
stepfather transference, he felt resentful toward
her and rejected. On a few occasions the patient
presented yet another resistance, a depressive
hopelessness and helplessness that probably hark-
ened back to loss of the mother in infancy. During
the periods when the patient was hopeless about
everything, including therapy, the therapist developed another countertransference resistance of
feeling hopeless about treating her.

The therapist's countertransference resistance flared up again and again because it plugged into a similar situation in his own childhood. His father had been an alcoholic who had battered his mother, and he had been the child who had been caught between. His mother, like this patient now, had continually complained to him about the father, but each time he had tried to intervene, his mother pushed him away and would forgive the father and reunite with him. Meanwhile, he had felt guilty about siding with the mother and in terror of the father.

In the therapy relationship, all these feelings from childhood came to the fore, giving added strength to the countertransference resistance. Instead of being a sympathetic listener who would give this patient the time and space to build up enough ego strength so that she could understand what was happening to her and leave her abusive spouse, he got embroiled in her situation. He hated the spouse and then felt guilty and terrified of him. He wanted to rescue the patient and then felt enraged when she continually failed to carry out the plans they both made for her to leave her spouse.

His countertransference resistance jarred against her resistance, and the patient and therapist became locked in a power struggle, which happens when resistance and counterresistance collide. Therapist wanted the patient to be a "good patient" and leave her mean husband; time and time again she said she would leave, but at the last minute she would come in with a new black eye and a new story of outrage. He gave new orders and she defied them. Soon her feelings of hopelessness grew worse and she developed a negative therapeutic reaction.

"I feel like I'm getting worse," she told him over and over. "I'm more depressed than I've ever been in my life. I can't sleep at night. I'm a wreck all day. My dentist says the bones in my jaw are deteriorating. My doctor says if I don't stop smoking so much I'll die of lung cancer. I don't feel like getting out of bed in the morning. I don't feel like working. I don't feel like doing anything. And I wonder whether the therapy is doing any good. Maybe I ought to go to a woman therapist. I mean, I've been seeing you for four years now and nothing's happening. I can't leave my husband and I don't understand why I can't leave him. Do you understand? If you do, why won't you tell me?"

His counterresistance had, in effect, pushed her into this negative therapeutic reaction. His message to her was, "When are you going to leave your husband? When? When?" Not that he would say this to her with words, but with his tone of voice and silences. He had a need to defend against the reemergence of the feelings of betrayal, rage, and hopelessness he experienced with respect to his mother by making it go right this time, and when he could not he felt guilty and further enraged. His impatience with the patient continually aroused her defiance. In her eyes he became more and more the intrusive, lustful stepfather, as evidenced by dreams in which he invaded her apartment and raped her. She felt pressured and blamed by him, so she in turned blamed him and pressured him. It was his fault that she could not leave her husband. He should have helped her more by now.

Eventually, with the help of supervision, this therapist was able to resolve his countertransference resistance and retreat to a more neutral position. Once he had done that, the patient began slowly to improve. To be sure, this kind of patient is difficult for any therapist, novice or veteran, and also for the people around her—friends, family, and community. It takes years of painstaking work to help a patient build up the ego strength required to individuate from such a spouse.

## HELPING THE PATIENT INTEGRATE DISOWNED PARTS

Racker (1968) points out that in order for a therapist to cure a patient he must help the patient integrate "ego alien" parts. All patients disown parts of themselves in one way or another—either through splitting, projection, reaction formation, repression, or another defense. In order to help the patient to integrate, the therapist must be fairly well integrated and thereby able to tolerate, in the countertransference, being the recipient of the patient's disowned parts. "The analyst is able to do this to the degree to which he has mastered his own ego defenses, and insofar as he is able to recognize what there is or was of himself in the patient" (p. 174).

Just as the patient's positive transference contributes to the working alliance, so also the therapist's positive countertransference contributes to this alliance. And if the therapist develops a negative countertransference, the alliance is adversely affected. When a therapist does develop a negative countertransference (as did the therapist in the last case with the battered woman), it is partially because of a failure to integrate his or her own disowned parts. The therapist in that case had not completely resolved his feelings of betrayal, guilt, and rage at his mother, nor the guilt and terror he felt toward his father, nor the feelings he had internalized, and had lodged in his own superego, to pass judgments about himself. All of these things, therefore, were still disowned by him, hence unconscious, hence able to be transferred onto patients. Whatever we are not conscious of, whatever we disown, is out of our control and subject to the whims of our defenses. (See Table 4–2.)

In addition, if we have not completely integrated ourselves, it is difficult for us to distinguish between objective and subjective countertransference. We can never know if the identification we feel with a patient is real or a projection of our disowned parts onto the patient (a projective identification). Nor can we distinguish between the patient's projective identification—and the feelings such identification arouse in us—and what our real feelings and attitudes are, for our disowned parts become aroused as well and all get mixed together. Or, as Racker noted, therapists may develop a complementary identification, in which they become so identified with what the patient is feeling that they become overly protective of the patient. In layman's terms, we take it personally when the patient treats us as though we were bad, has unrealistic expectations, or is critical of us, and we may become overinvolved if a patient appears too needy.

Just as the patient uses the transference resistance to relive the past and make it go right this

**Table 4–2.** Transference and Countertransference Resistance

| Character of Patient | Type of Resistance | Type of Counter-resistance | Function of Counter-resistance |
|---|---|---|---|
| Obsessive-Compulsive | Passive-aggression | Angry interpretations of patient's behavior | Defend against memories of childhood frustrations |
| Hysterical | Seductive manipulation | Flirting with or sexually rejecting patient | Defend against oedipal memories |
| Masochistic | Spiteful defiance | Hostile interpretations; attempts to control patient | Defend against anal memories |
| Narcissistic | Idealization/devaluation | Idealization and devaluation of patient | Defend against memories of devaluation and scorn |
| Paranoid | Tyrannical manipulation | Hostile efforts to control or get rid of patient | Defend against primitive fears of reengulfment, annihilation |
| Depressive | Hopelessness, rejection of therapist and self | Hopelessness about reaching patient; rejection of patient | Defend against oral memories |
| Schizophrenic | Withdrawal from therapist | Efforts to draw patient out with kindness; symbiotic clinging; murderous rage | Defend against memories of childhood loss |

time, so too the therapist attempts through the countertransference resistance to defend against and relive in a better way the original traumatic situation. If a therapist can experience the counter-transference feelings and objectify them (and not act them out through some kind of resistance), they can be used to understand the patient's trans-ference defenses and identifications; however, if the therapist cannot objectify the countertransfer-ence feelings, they will become countertransfer-ence resistances. This, again, points up the impor-tance for therapists to analyze themselves first, and then their patients. Nor should they be reticent about seeking help by way of more supervision or analysis.

I recall someone in a supervision group pre-senting a case and then saying, "I hope it's not my countertransference."

"What if it is?" I replied.

"Then I'm in trouble."

Often, those who become therapists do so in order to attain some kind of certification that they are sane. Their therapeutic training becomes a formality for getting this certification, and they only pretend to take stock of themselves and their own resistances. Later, after they have gotten their diplomas and graduated from psychoanalytic or psychotherapy institutes, they develop a feeling of therapeutic infallibility. After all, they are the ones with the diplomas on the wall.

Sometimes the most effective supervision and training happens after formal training has been completed.

# 5

# Characterological Counterresistance

Characterological counterresistance, in contrast to countertransference resistance, is related to the character of the therapist. This kind of resistance by the therapist does not necessarily arise in connection with anything the patient says or does, but is the characteristic way a therapist expresses himself in all aspects of his life. It is often related to the therapist's repetition compulsion, and is designed to help him bind anxiety and defend against the eruption of ego-dystonic memories, thoughts, wishes, and impulses. In the characterological resistance there is an even greater emphasis on reversing what was traumatic in childhood, turning the tables on those who are perceived to be threatening as a way of maintaining homeostasis.

Racker (1968) was the first to refer to characterological counterresistances, observing that "a study of such character disturbances in the analyst and his corresponding countertransference would be of great practical value" (p. 177). He noted that therapists could develop a countertransference neurosis, analogous to the patient's transference neurosis. He also examined psychoanalysts' "unconscious masochism" and "unconscious mania" and showed how they affected the therapy process.

Glover (1955), alluded to the therapeutic implications of the analyst's character when he stated, "Everything the analyst thinks, says or does during the countertransference can, where necessary or expedient, be self-interpreted as counterresistance" (p. 98). He also seemed to be hinting at the problem of character resistances when he referred to the dangers that occur when an analyst develops what he called a "fetishistic" allegiance to transference interpretation (p. 130).

Fromm-Reichmann (1950), without using the word counterresistance detailed a number of attitudes and traits by psychotherapists that impede their work. For example, she pointed out that "insecure and self-righteous psychiatrists cannot endure their failure to understand patients' communications without developing feelings of anxiety or resentment" (p. 18). She concluded that "where there is anxiety, there is a fear of the anxieties of others. The insecure psychiatrist is, therefore, liable to be afraid of his patients' anxiety" (p. 24). She explained that such analysts might thwart patients' tendencies to submit these experiences to psychotherapeutic investigation by giving premature reassurance to patients due to a need to reassure themselves. They thereby end up obstructing (resisting) the patients' verbalizations and fore-stalling the investigation of important material.

Reich (1933), who founded character analysis, provided extensive instructions on the analysis of his patient's character resistances, which he called "character armor." However, he examined only briefly the character resistances of psychoanalysts. "Quite obviously, the ability of the analyst to adopt a flexible attitude in his work, to grasp the case intuitively without becoming stuck in his intellectually acquired knowledge, will depend upon conditions pertaining to his character in the same way that the similar ability of the analysand to let himself go is determined by the degree to which his character armor has been loosened" (p. 147). He referred to the analyst's narcissism noting that "analysts who experience the transferences of their patients in an essentially narcissistic way tend to interpret those contemporary manifestations of love as signs of a personal love relationship" (p. 149). Likewise, he warned that analysts who had not "gotten in control of their sadism" could lapse into analytic silence and use that to frustrate patients whom they regard "as an enemy who does not want to get well" (p. 149).

In Reich's day it was assumed that psychoanalysts had only minimal character resistances; anybody who was successfully analyzed was believed to have worked through such things. However, in the years since, the profession has come to realize that, in a sense, psychoanalysis is never finished, and this applies to both regular and training analyses. Psychoanalysts, like patients, have character resistances. Since there is no such thing as a truly completed training analysis, nor a perfect human being, this goes without saying. But it is assumed that psychoanalysts are at least more in touch with their resistances than patients. At any rate, the character resistances of both patients and analysts must be analyzed if a therapy is to be successful, and more often than not, as I stated earlier, it is the analyst's unconscious and unanalyzed resistances that are responsible for failure.


## FREUD AND THE WOLF MAN

Sigmund Freud's treatment of the Wolf Man serves as an illustration of the problem of characterological counterresistance. Freud's initial analysis of the Wolf Man lasted four years—from February 1910 until the summer of 1914, and was by far the longest analysis undergone until that time. In writing up this case (1918), Freud acknowledged several deviations from standard technique: giving direct advice (at first advising the Wolf Man not to marry and then later advising him to marry), meeting the patient's fiancée, accepting an expensive termination gift (an Egyptian antiquity), providing free analytic sessions and giving the patient money. After three and a half years Freud decided to set a termination date for the analysis (another deviation) because it had been at an impasse for a year, and he hoped the threat of termination would force the patient out of his resistance. This intervention did serve to bring up new material in the next six months, but left much unfinished. Freud seemed to be anxious to complete the case so that he could write about it.

The Wolf Man was to return to Freud briefly a second time after he had lost his fortune following the Russian Revolution in 1918 (he was of the Russian upper class), and then he ultimately went into psychoanalysis with Ruth Mack Brunswick. During this second analysis a full-blown paranoia erupted in which he believed he was Christ and that both Freud and Brunswick were conspiring against him. He threatened to kill them both until Brunswick succeeded in interpreting his transference psychosis.

Numerous psychoanalysts have since commented on Freud's countertransference in this case. Rosenfeld (1956), citing Freud's obsession with the Wolf Man's primal scene (i.e., his attempt to prove the existence of one with only indirect and inconclusive evidence), wondered if Freud may have been troubled by counteridentifications, mixing reactions to his own primal scene with that of the Wolf Man's and hoping to recover his own primal scene in that way. He points out that during Freud's early childhood his parents lived in a one-room apartment, and he would most likely have witnessed their intercourse.

Blum (1980) asserts that Freud misdiagnosed the Wolf Man as an obsessive-compulsive, when, in fact, he was suffering from a severe borderline disturbance. He explains that the Wolf Man's development of a transference psychosis toward Brunswick fourteen years after his treatment with Freud had ended reflected a typical borderline lack

of true ego-integration and the consequent vulner-
ability to regression under stress.

Langs (1980) suggests that there were problems in Freud's therapeutic alliance with the Wolf
Man. Freud's double interest in the Wolf Man, as
both patient and research subject (and the fact that
he made this interest known to the latter), as well
as his fixed termination date, represented a kind of
acting out that engendered a misalliance in which
"Freud became the God (father), who promised a
cure and who brought matters to an end (death),
and in which the Wolf Man became the victim,
Christ" (p. 375). This resulted in a transference
cure rather than a real cure, one that gratified the
Wolf Man's narcissistic needs.

What all of these critiques seem to point to is
how Freud's own obsessive-compulsive character
resistances impeded the therapy. That Freud had
obsessive-compulsive features in his personality is
readily evident from biographical data about his
life. For example, to name a few, he had a lifelong
obsession with psychoanalysis and with fame; indeed he never seemed to stop thinking and wor-
rying about both. One might also argue that his
prolific writings and tendency toward all work and
no play served as a ritual, much like the repeated
washing of the hands does for typical obsessive-
compulsives, to stave off the eruption of repressed
oedipal guilt and sexual and aggressive impulses.
Other symptoms include his penchant for orderli-
ness, apparent in his manner of dress, in his life-
style, and in his way of doing therapy. Then there
was his collecting of antiquities, which was excessive and could be seen as a kind of hoarding.

As an obsessive-compulsive, he was prone to being overly zealous about certain ideas and not letting them go. He apparently frightened Dora away, partly because he had a fetish with interpreting her dreams even when she demonstrated that she was not ready to hear them (1905). In the Wolf Man's case, he persisted in trying to prove a primal scene for which there was not a single memory or any other clear evidence. His misdiagnosis of the Wolf Man as an obsessive-compulsive was also possibly due to a character resistance; his need to keep his own primal impulses suppressed prevented him from being able to tolerate the primal borderline feelings of others, including the Wolf Man, and to misdiagnose them. Also, due to his compulsivity, he had a need to impose clarity and order on the case as soon as possible. When the Wolf Man did not cooperate with this need but instead stubbornly resisted Freud's attempts, Freud did not have the patience or the proper empathic attunement to deal with him. The Wolf Man's stubborn silence aroused a counterresistance, and Freud "acted out" by setting the termination date. Indeed, that the Wolf Man had fallen into a stubborn silence raises the question of what Freud had done to cause him to lapse into the silence in the first place. Had he done so because Freud was continually guiding the therapy, attempting to fit the Wolf Man into his preconceived ideas about him?

Long after the termination, Freud continued to obsess about his emphasis on the primal scene in the Wolf Man's case. He did not publish it for four years, and, when he did, he wrote in a footnote, "I admit that this is the most ticklish question in the whole domain of psychoanalysis. . . . No other uncertainty has been more decisive in holding me back from publishing my conclusions." When he published the case (1916–1917), he cited still more evidence for the existence of the primal scene, speculating that such memories "were once real occurrences in the primaeval time of the human family, and . . . children in their fantasies are simply filling in gaps in individual truth with historical truth" (p. 371).

That Freud had a resistance to working with more disturbed patients is well known, but that this resistance was due to his obsessive-compulsive character has not, to my knowledge, been duly noted. Stolorow and Atwood (1979) explored Freud's theories in light of his "subjective representational world" and concluded that "Freud's wish to restore and preserve an early idealized image of his mother ran through his life like a red thread, influencing his reconstructions of his early childhood history, his choice of a field of study, his important adult relationships, and his theoretical ideas" (p. 68). However, they did not classify him as an obsessive-compulsive. There is, shall we say, a resistance to using such diagnostic terms for analysts; that is to say, there is a resistance to uncovering and labeling a resistance. But unless we do so, we cannot hope to work successfully with patients.

## JUNG AND THE PHILOSOPHY STUDENT

In Carl Jung's case, it was his schizophrenic characterological resistances that impeded his work as a therapist. Stern (1976) called Jung a "haunted prophet" whose psychotic episodes during his youth led to his later formulating theoretical ideas that were tainted by mysticism and magical thinking. During his youth, Jung became convinced that he was two people—a lonely, only child who was tyrannized by his mother, cut off from his father, and isolated from schoolmates, and a powerful and wise old man who lived in the previous century, wore buckled shoes and a white wig, and knew secrets others did not know. Stern interpreted that Jung was haunted by oedipal anger and guilt toward his father, which got transferred onto Freud and influenced his alternatingly submissive and rebellious attitude toward the latter. Jung's theoretical dismissal of the Oedipus complex and of infantile sexuality was due to pregenital fixations, and his obsession with religion and philosophy was both a way of clinging to his mother, who had encouraged him in that direction, and a way of holding on to his second personality, the wise old man, which was in reality a schizophrenic delusion.

His case history of his analysis with the philosophy student (1971) illustrates how his schizoid character resistances prevented him from working successfully with her. The philosophy student entered treatment in 1910 (the same year that Freud began treating the Wolf Man), and he diagnosed her as suffering from "a mild hysterical neurosis," the principal cause of which was a "father-complex." The philosophy student complained to Jung that she could never find a man who was on her intellectual level, like her father had been. However, her repeating pattern was of controlling

and devaluing the men she dated. Jung soon
learned that she had been her father's favorite; she
had taken the mother's place in his heart and had
been his "supremely wise, very grown-up, all-
understanding mother-daughter-beloved" (p. 108).
When the patient transferred the "father imago"
onto Jung and began first to critize him and then to
idealize him as a "savior or a god," he tried to
analyze her father transference. When she persisted in this positive transference toward him and
came in each day in great spirits, he became uncomfortable and did not know what to do next. He
suggested that since she was feeling better, they
should terminate therapy. She protested, saying
she would be terrified to leave therapy at that
point. He insisted, saying that she could not remain
dependent on him forever.

By now the patient had run out of money and
he was seeing her at no charge. Searching for an
answer, Jung suggested that she bring in dreams
as a way of breaking the transference deadlock.
One day she brought in a dream that typified and
crystallized the themes that ran through all the
dreams: Her father was standing with her on a hill
that was covered with wheat. She was quite tiny
beside him, and he seemed to her like a giant. He
lifted her up from the ground and held her in his
arms like a little child. The wind swept over the
wheat fields, and, as the wheat swayed with the
wind, he rocked her in his arms.

Jung interpreted this dream as a wish to make
him into "a doctor of superhuman proportions, a
gigantic primordial father, a god who is at the same
time the wind, and in whose protecting arms you

are resting like an infant" (p. 79). He gave the patient a lengthy explanation of archetypes and mysticism and mythology, asserting that her dream had come from the collective unconscious and was a divine oracle sent from above to help her resolve her father transference. The philosophy student was skeptical, protesting that she found his earlier interpretation about her father complex more appealing. She proceeded to bring in more and more dreams in which the father was swelled to even grander proportions, but at the same time she began a new relationship with a man and started to pull away from Jung. Soon he set a termination date, and he reported that when it came, "it was no catastrophe, but a perfectly reasonable parting" (p. 79).

Jung made many glaring errors in this case, and it appears that his own withdrawn, mystical, schizophrenic character was at the root of these errors. He was resistant to the erotic elements of the patient's oedipal transference to him and over-emphasized the narcissistic elements—her overvaluation of him. Because of his fear of her erotic attachment to him, and perhaps because of his irritation at her criticisms, he tried early on to get rid of her, telling her that since she was feeling better it was a good time for her to terminate. That she responded with terror to this suggestion shows how far Jung was out of attunement with the patient. Next he tried to get rid of her by interpreting her dreams as attempts to make him into a god and giving her lengthy, abstract lectures about mysticism and mythology. She replied that she liked his previous interpretations about her father transference better than his talks about gods and archetypes, but he did not properly understand her, and he persisted. When the patient began another affair and started pulling away from Jung, he interpreted this as the work of the collective unconscious and as a kind of divine intervention. He again suggested termination and this time it was "a perfectly reasonable parting." Most likely he had induced her to join his resistance and to pretend everything was for the best, when in fact she had probably become discouraged and resentful of his constant indifference to her attempts to get close to him.

Jung's efforts to divert the patient's attention into mystical thinking represented not only a resistance to her erotic transference, but also to the aggression that lurked beneath, which was manifested by her critical attitude toward him in the beginning of the therapy. Treating her at no charge was also a resistance; he might well have ended the therapy on this basis rather than suggesting that she quit because she was feeling better. His refusal to do so belies a reluctance on his part to confront the aggression behind her supposed lack of funds and the possible wish that he would view her on a personal rather than professional basis. This reluctance to confront her erotic and aggressive drives probably had to do with his unresolved feelings about his mother, whom he had split into two people when he was a boy, the good mother and the monster. He had not worked through his erotic or aggressive feelings about his monster-mother and hence he could not help his patient work through her erotic and aggressive feelings toward him.

Thompson (1950), critiquing Jung's brand of dream interpretation, was skeptical. "One cannot help thinking that in spite of the interpretation, the patient's problem still remains but thinking about something else has been substituted for it" (p. 169). Jung's own tendencies toward depersonalization and splitting impelled him to encourage his patients in the same direction. The danger of this, Thompson pointed out, was that it took patients away from reality toward "a mystical, semi-religious fantasy life" that might well exacerbate, rather than resolve, their problems, especially those prone to "autistic thinking" (p. 169).

## REICH AND THE MASOCHISTIC PATIENT

There is a good reason why Wilhelm Reich's work on masochism and his delineation of the masoch-istic character structure stand out even today. He himself had strong masochistic features in his personality (among other trends), and his life as well as his work are manifestations of this masoch-ism.

Not much is known about his early childhood except that he grew up on a farm in Austria and claimed to have no friends outside his family. His father is said to have been a sadistic, authoritarian man, given to violent outbursts of temper. His mother was supposedly an attractive but not very intelligent person, who enjoyed the attention of other men, and his father was possessive and jealous of other men's interests in her. Reich had a strong attachment to the mother and competed for her favor throughout his childhood with his brother, who was three years younger. A major trauma occurred when he was 14. He found out that his mother was having an affair with his tutor, and immediately informed his father. His mother then killed herself.

Stolorow and Atwood (1979) speculated that Reich's guilt over his mother's suicide underpinned his lifelong struggle against sexual repression. "In acting on the basis of a narrow code of sexual morality, he was responsible for the death of the one person he loved above all others" (p. 121). His attempt to inhibit his beloved mother's sexuality had led directly to her suicide. His crusade against antisexual death forces (whether they be character armor, fascism, T-bacilli, or invading space creatures) was indicative of a strong paranoid trend as well as of a masochistic ethos. Other examples of his masochistic character structure were his continual complaints of being mistreated and misunderstood, a certain arrogance in his personality and boastfulness in his writings that provoked contempt, causing Freud and nearly all of the psychoanalytic community to reject him, and provocative research projects that got him kicked out of one country after another (and resulted in his being investigated for quackery in America and eventually imprisoned).

In his writings he suggested that analysts be restrained in handling the negative transference so as not to discourage its full development in the treatment, asserting that if the patient was left to determine for himself the number and timing of interventions, the transference would unfold. How-

ever, in his case history about the masochistic
patient he began almost from the outset to provoke
the patient's negative transference.

The patient, a young loner who fantasized
about wandering through the woods devising a
mathematical system that would save the world,
maintained a facade of being composed and well-
bred. Reich lost no time in interpreting this facade.
"It serves as a compensation for your feeling of
complete worthlessness, a feeling intimately related to and continually reproduced by your experience of masturbation as something dirty and
squalid" (1933, p. 239). As Reich interpreted this
facade, the patient began to become defiant. The
patient would come in complaining about being in
a masochistic bog. Reich would ask him to elabo-
rate, and the patient would say, "No, I won't." If
Reich insisted, the patient would repeat, "No, I
won't, I won't, I won't." The patient, Reich concluded, was attempting to reduce his therapeutic
efforts to absurdity. For the first six months they
were locked in a struggle of wills. He would open
the door and find the patient standing there each
day "with a sullen, pain-distorted, spongy face, the
epitome of a bundle of misery" (p. 244). Reich
began to mirror the patient, putting on the exact
same face himself. When the patient said, "I
won't," Reich echoed "I won't." The patient grew
enraged, and one day he began kicking and
screaming on the couch. "Do that again," Reich
said. The patient was astounded by this request,
but did so. As he kicked and screamed, Reich
interpreted his behavior, saying he did not really
hate Reich, he hated his father.

This, according to Reich, was a turning point in the analysis. As the treatment continued, the masochist would consume entire hours with kicking and screaming and began to enjoy it. Reich now ascertained that the patient had become stuck in this screaming and kicking stage; he enjoyed being bad because it repeated a phase of behavior he had gone through from the ages of 4 to 5. To break this new impasse, Reich got on the floor and began kicking and screaming alongside the patient. The patient gawked at him, stopped what he was doing, and laughed. "I continued these procedures until he himself began to analyze" (p. 244). From that time on, according to Reich, the analysis proceeded without a hitch, and Reich described how he cured the masochist by encouraging him to achieve orgiastic potency.

The case sounds successful, yet appearances can be deceiving. When the case was presented in a paper for publication in the *International Journal of Psycho-Analysis* of 1932, Freud, who was then the editor, at first did not wish to publish it. He was not only disturbed by Reich's deviation from standard technique, but also by his repudiation of the death instinct theory. Thompson (1950) also took issue with "much of Reich's thinking" in the paper, and she pointed out that most analysts were not as active as Reich, preferring to treat character trends "like other neurotic symptoms. Insight into them is to be presented to the patient only when he is ready for it and can therefore utilize the knowledge constructively" (p. 190).

Since Reich does not provide any follow-up on this case, we have no way of knowing whether the cure was lasting. However, it seems likely that it was not. Rather, like Freud's treatment of the Wolf Man and Jung's work with the philosophy student, this case has the markings of a transference cure. Although I believe that the patient determines the treatment, and my own work tends to be eclectic, nevertheless I have discovered that too much activity, like too much silence, can be a resistance to "going with the flow." By pressing, you seem to get things moving faster and the patient makes quick strides toward success, but this can be an illusion, as was later evident in the case of the Wolf Man.

One detects not neutrality in Reich's attitude toward his patient, but ridicule and contempt. He describes the patient as having a "sullen, pain-distorted, spongy face, the epitome of a bundle of misery," and tells how he imitates that face and parrots his "I won't." Prior to that he describes in great detail how and when the patient masturbates, and notes that when he ejaculated "semen did not spurt out rhythmically but merely flowed out" (p. 238). For him to have attained such detailed information about the patient's ejaculation would have required him to ask very pointed questions about it, which may very likely have felt intrusive to the patient, as well as possibly seductive. He has the patient kick and scream and gets down and kicks and screams with him. In and of itself, this technique is not wrong; it is the tenor of the technique. The overall picture here is of a patient who is being forced to submit (in a passive-homosexual-masochistic way) to Reich's anal-sadistic domination. The patient gives himself to this new surrogate father and gets well for him. But

has he really worked through his feelings, or
merely acted them out in the transference? And
what about his pregenital feelings toward his
mother? Not much is said about them.

It appears that Reich's sadomasochistic character structure made him intolerant of the patient's
similar characterology, and impelled him to
quickly attack it. He did not have the patience to
allow the patient's material to evolve at its own
pace. His need to dominate and control the patient,
to act out his own unconscious oedipal fear of being
brutalized by his father (reversing roles here in the
countertransference), as well as his need to com-
pensate for guilt feelings about his sexual desire
for, and murderous wishes about, his mother,
seemingly took precedence over the patient's
needs. He imposed his own agenda on the patient,
guiding him toward genital potency rather than
letting him find his own way to homeostasis.
Acting out this male rite of passage undoubtedly
offered secondary gratification to both therapist
and patient, but it may also have been "full of
sound and fury, signifying nothing."

## SUBTLER VARIETIES OF
## CHARACTEROLOGICAL
## COUNTERRESISTANCE

The cases I have cited are all from the beginning
days of psychoanalysis, when analytic technique
had not been refined and analysts did not undergo
lengthy training analyses. Today's psychoanalysts
and psychotherapists are more thoroughly ana-

lyzed and supervised, and their characterological resistance may be of a more subtle variety. However, even though therapists today are more thoroughly trained, that training may have minimal impact on characterological counterresistances.

Analytic and psychotherapeutic trainees tend to choose as training analysts and supervisors people who have similar characterological and cultural resistances. Thus, their resistances may be given scant attention and are often seen as strengths, rather than resistances. In the rare instances when trainees do not end up with characterologically or culturally similar analysts and supervisors, they may not be receptive to their feedback, and while there is an effort to focus on the trainee's typical characterological resistances, that effort is not always successful.

Today's therapists still have characterological resistances, but their manifestations may not be as dramatic as the ones I have cited. They are more apt to be of a more routine variety—subtle silences or slightly incorrect or ill-timed interpretations. For example, a female analyst may notice that a woman patient is too dependent on her husband, which arouses countertransference feelings. The analyst interprets the patient's dependency, linking it to her relationship with her father, who cultivated such a dependency in her. In subsequent sessions the patient reports that she has thought about the interpretation and finds herself depending less and less on her husband, and she provides examples of this liberation. Yet there is something unreal about the way she is talking. What has happened, in fact, is that the patient was not ready to hear this interpretation, and hence felt accused by the therapist. She reacted by complying to the suggestion behind the interpretation (don't be so dependent) in order to win her therapist's approval. But, in fact, the patient is worse off than before, for her alliance with the therapist has become more defended and less trusting.

The therapist in this case was resistant to allowing the treatment to evolve naturally. She heard dependency in the patient's descriptions of her relationship with her husband, and because of her own unresolved oral-dependency needs, was compelled to venture this interpretation. If analysts have not achieved true independence—if they continue to struggle against or give in to needs because they have not worked through them in their own analyses—they cannot react appropriately to patients. When one's internal objects are in harmony, one does not need to defend against, rearrange, or overreact to external ones.

Not only words and silences, but also gestures can stem from characterological counterresistances. For example, one therapist had a smile on her face each time a patient arrived and left her office. This smile was rooted in her hysterical character—she was a hysteric of the "Pollyanna" variety who had a need to deny her own and other people's aggression and fear of confrontation. Through her training analysis and supervision she had learned all about these tendencies and fears, and she attempted to overcome them by pointedly encouraging her patients to tell her any negative thoughts they might have about her; but these suggestions were in contrast to the smile she flashed before and after each session, which seemed to say, "Let's keep everything on a friendly basis and not say anything that might hurt each other." Hence, her patients would be put into a double bind; her words said "do," her smile said "don't." Quite unconsciously and unwittingly the therapist resisted the patients' negative feelings while pretending to encourage them, the result being that patients either formed a Pollyanna collusion with her and made only superficial progress or became convinced they had improved and left therapy. Unfortunately, therapists do not generally describe their routine smiles to their supervisors, so this kind of counterresistance is difficult to detect.

Finally, one of the most common characterological counterresistances of psychoanalysts relates to their narcissism. In many psychoanalysts this narcissism takes the form of an elitist, scholarly attitude. In their writings and lectures, such analysts go to great lengths to demonstrate their understanding of metapsychology, and they outdo each other in their use of the most obtuse and esoteric language. Marshall (1991) wryly notes how such analysts are prone to immersing themselves in metapsychological phrases like "the reaggressivised energy of the countercathexes" (Hartmann 1950, p. 134) and "the dedifferentiating influx of unneutralized narcissistic libido" (Kohut 1978, p. 152), when simpler language might be both more accessible and more understandable. They of course firmly believe they are trying to make psychoanalysis more precise and more scientific, but in fact they are making it more complicated and

**Table 5–1.**  Characterological Counterresistances

| Character of Therapist | What is Resisted | Major Defense Mechanism | Characteristic Means of Resistance |
|---|---|---|---|
| Obsessive-Compulsive | Resists disorder, spontaneity, tenderness, craziness | Undoing childhood shame (defense against soiling) | Passive–aggressive frustration of patient |
| Hysterical | Resists sexual and aggressive themes | Denial (defense against envy and sexual aggression) | Seductive manipulation of patient |
| Masochistic | Resists self-assertion | Displacement of anger, shame and guilt | Victory through humility |
| Narcissistic | Resists devaluation | Splitting (defense against scorn) | Grandiose alliance with patient; intellectualism |
| Paranoid | Resists persecution, thought control | Splitting, projection (defense against self-destruction) | Tyranny over patient |
| Depressive | Resists love, respect, happiness | Self-devaluation (anger turned inward) | Guilty overconcern or rejection of patient |
| Schizophrenic | Resists self-annihilation, murderous wishes | Dissociation, depersonalization, hallucination (defense against murderous rage) | Delusional alliance with patient; symbiotic clinging |

quasiscientific. To many outside the field of psychoanalysis, incessant babble about metapsychology is likened to astrological writings about rising signs and stars. To make it really scientific, we must bring it back to earth, back to what we can more clearly observe and document, and to make it really accessible rather than avoidant, we should write in language that reaches the heart as well as the intellect.

Understanding ourselves is a step in this direction. There are many characterological counterresistances, and intellectualization is one of them. To familiarize ourselves with ourselves is our most pertinent challenge. (See Table 5–1 on characterological counterresistances.)

Lao Tzu's notion "To know yourself is to know all," is certainly relevant to psychoanalysis. But the narcissistic part protests, "That's old stuff. I know all that. But what about the patient's reaggressivised unneutralized dedifferentiated countercathexis? Tell me more about that."

# 6

# Cultural Counterresistance

Perhaps nowhere more than in America do ethnic and cultural issues come up in therapy. We have become increasingly diverse, drawing people of varying ethnic and cultural backgrounds into our society, with the result that our society is far from homogeneous. Not only the patients but we ourselves are from differing origins with differing belief systems and values. Clearly when our backgrounds, belief systems, or values clash with those of our patients, there will be problems.

Moreover, there is at present and always has been ongoing social strife among the various races and subraces, ethnic groups, political groups, economic classes, religions, and ideologies. This strife results in an ever-shifting miasma of cultural values, which in turn affects each individual in society, including those individuals in therapy and those doing it.

Of all the resistances, cultural resistances and counterresistances are often the most pervasive and rigid while being the least understood. They are unwittingly ignored by both patient and therapist and become destructive to the therapy process. We are much more reluctant to confront a patient's religious beliefs or political ideology or racial biases, even though they may be resistances, than we are to confront characterological resistance. We are even more reluctant to look at our own. Indeed, we may be so caught up in our biases that we do not think of them as such nor do we see how they hinder the therapy process. Sometimes we even assume them to be beneficial, (as when we harbor the belief that everyone should be as liberal as we are).

## CULTURAL VALUES AND THERAPY

Critics of Freud unwittingly point out one of his chief cultural counterresistances when they allude to his Victorian ideas. They maintain that his Victorianism affects not only his theories about women, but also his therapy with them. They cite cases such as that of "Dora," in which Freud seemed to side with the father, his friend, viewing Dora's situation from her father's (and the male) point of view, while failing to empathize with Dora's point of view. The Victorian age was in fact a patriarchal time; fathers were seen as "right," and the feelings and thoughts of daughters were not taken seriously. Freud, being a product of that culture, harbored a cultural counterresistance that stood in the way of his being able to assist Dora and other female patients as well as he might have.

Cultural resistances and counterresistances are actually cultural biases that become resistances to intimacy. Such biases generally serve to maintain some form of dogma, and hence they prevent genuine relating while maintaining an artificial balance of power or privilege. The ideology of Victorianism, for example, maintained the superiority of men over women and thus kept women sexually and emotionally repressed, preventing a healthy relationship between men and women. Cultural resistances and counterresistances can be of several varieties: ideological, religious, political, racial, ethnic, sexual, regional, or national.

Religious beliefs can become cultural resistances, as when therapists are "married to God" and therefore cannot understand or bond with a secular patient, or when therapists' religious views make them intolerant to a patient's beliefs. Political views can become resistances, as when a liberal therapist unconsciously (or consciously) disapproves of a conservative patient's views (or vice versa) and therefore resists hearing what he or she is saying or empathizing with it. White therapists might unconsciously resist black patients in various ways. If the therapist is a white liberal, he or she may develop a reaction formation toward the patient, disowning any negative thoughts or feelings out of a fear of coming across as prejudiced; in doing so, the therapist robs the relationship of genuineness and keeps it on a false level. Male therapists may harbor unconscious sexist attitudes toward females, and female therapists may have biased feminist attitudes toward males. Northern therapists may disaprove of and resist Southerners, and American therapists may resent and resist Japanese-American patients.

One of the more prevalent and destructive forms of cultural counterresistance comes about when therapists identify their ideal selves with a cause, religion, or mass movement. Such people generally become self-righteous, utilizing the cause or movement to back up their narcissism or masochism. Joining with many others, they feel right through group consensus and are convinced that others, the movement's scapegoats, are wrong. This enables them to justify the transferring, resisting, and acting out of resistances to such outsiders without feeling guilt. In these cases, the cause, religion, or movement becomes a narcissistic extension of the therapist's ideal image, while those parts of their selves that they wish to disown are projected onto outsiders; they and their movement are good and outsiders and their movements are bad. In the therapy dyad, when a therapist treats a patient who appears to be an outsider, the therapist may unconsciously resist certain material from this patient that the therapist considers bad or politically incorrect, thereby derailing the therapeutic process. Frequently the therapist and patient will be from the same movement, and hence will form a collusion that prevents (resists and counterresists) real therapeutic work.

It might be argued that the resistance I am describing as a cultural resistance is in actuality an aspect of character. Our beliefs, so this argument goes, are an outgrowth of our character and our upbringing. Hence, religiosity might be an aspect of an obsessive-compulsive or masochistic characterology, while racial bias might be seen as stemming from an identification with racially biased parents. However, there are some cases where a temporary cultural trend, such as the Nazi movement in pre-World War II Germany or the McCarthyism of 1950s America, will sweep across a society and affect all of its members. If there were any therapists during the Nazi era, they most likely would have had a cultural counterresistance when it came to treating Jews or Germans suspected of being sympathizers. Similarly, a therapist during the McCarthy era might have had a bias toward any patient who expressed anything resembling a communist viewpoint. Counterresistances of this type would not be the product of child-rearing but would be induced by the currents of the times. Hence I have made a distinction between characterological and cultural resistances and counterresistances even though I recognize some overlapping.

Like other resistances, cultural resistances and counterresistances defend against the hazards of intimacy. A therapist during the McCarthy era, for example, treating a patient he suspected of being a communist, might have been driven by a terror of being contaminated by the patient's communism. Such a therapist might have picked up the emotional contagion of the times, and, like McCarthy, disowned the evil in himself and projected it onto the patient. Through projective identification, the patient would be viewed as a secret terrorist out to overthrow not only the country, but also the therapist himself. There might also be fears of guilt by association with this patient. (See Table 6–1.)

## EXCLUSION AND COLLUSION

In considering the various types of cultural counterresistances that can invade the therapy relationship, it is easier to explore those that happened in the past. We can look back on Nazism or McCarthyism or Victorianism with relative objectivity and readily see how such movements, along with their cultural values, might affect all individual relationships, including therapy ones. It is not so easy to look at present-day cultural factors, for we are much more involved in them and less objective. Yet, it is just as pertinent for the purposes of psychotherapy to be able to objectively analyze cultural counterresistances as it is any other type of counterresistance, and hence we must be willing to look at our own and our patients' biases. The main problem in doing this is that while our patients' biases may stand out clearly, our own biases often seem like the way things really are; they are ego-syntonic.

For example, a case came to my attention of a woman therapist from a conservative cultural background who did not believe in abortion. When one of her young women patients became pregnant and began discussing plans to have an abortion, the therapist found it difficult to remain neutral.

"I don't think it would be fair to try to raise a

**Table 6-1.** Cultural Counterresistances

| Bias of Therapist | What is Resisted | Major Defense Mechanisms | Method of Resisting |
|---|---|---|---|
| Religious | Resists opposing ideologies and religions | Splitting, projection, religious narcissism | Indoctrination of "heathen" patients; idealization of, collusion with religious patients |
| Ideological | Resists opposing religions and ideologies | Splitting, projection, ideological narcissism | Indoctrination of "enemy" patients; idealization of, collusion with ideological patients |
| Racial | Resists other races | Splitting, projection, reaction formation, racial narcissism | Character assassination of other races; idealization of, collusion with same race |
| Gender | Resists other gender | Splitting, projection, gender narcissism | Psychological castration of other sex patients; idealization of, collusion with same sex |
| Sexual Orientation | Resists other orientations | Splitting, projection, sexual orientation narcissism | Indoctrination guilt induction of other orientations; idealization of, collusion with own orientations |
| Regional | Resists other regions | Splitting, projection, regional narcissism | Devaluation of patients from other regions; idealization of collusion with own region |
| Class (economic, occupational) | Resists other classes | Splitting, projection, class narcissism | Devaluation of other classes; idealization of, collusion with own class |

baby alone," the patient mused. "I couldn't give the child the kind of attention it would need. I think abortion is really the only viable option."

"You seem to think that if you can't give the child a perfect childhood, you shouldn't have it," the therapist commented.

"No, that's not what I was saying." The patient looked at the therapist in surprise. "You're putting words in my mouth."

From the moment the patient became pregnant and began discussing abortion, the therapist found herself feeling angry at the patient and viewing her in a different light. She had grown up in a small-town Catholic culture in which women who had abortions were viewed as selfish, irresponsible, and promiscuous. Now, despite her therapeutic training, she found herself viewing this patient disparagingly, and, whenever the patient spoke about abortion, the therapist either went silent or put words in the patient's mouth. After the patient had the abortion, the therapist felt resentful toward her. Whereas she had once had a good relationship with her, it became distant and falsely cordial. Unconsciously, the therapist no longer wished to be close to the patient and she acted out this wish in subtle ways. Eventually the therapist's cultural counterresistance led to the patient's finding reasons to terminate therapy, which the therapist all too readily accepted.

Another case that came to my attention involved a male homosexual therapist and a male homosexual patient. The therapist believed that homosexuality was a genetic disorder and subscribed to current research with twins that seemed to support this theory. He had done his training analyses with other therapists, straight and gay, who also subscribed to these theories, and hence he had avoided dealing with his castration or Oedipus complexes in his own training.

His patient, however was not sure about whether homosexuality was genetically or environmentally produced, and he was conflicted about his homosexuality. Part of him wanted to be straight, to be married and have children, and to live a "normal life." In the beginning of the therapy, the patient talked a great deal about these conflicts. The therapist tried to listen and be supportive, but soon the patient stopped talking about these matters and concentrated on more superficial issues relating to his job. Still later, he found reasons to quit therapy.

It was only after he had lost the patient that the therapist realized, in talking with his supervision group, that his cultural counterresistance had come into play. Even though he had not said anything to the patient with regard to his beliefs, he had expressed them in other ways. For example, whenever the patient had talked about his homosexual impulses, the therapist asked many questions and showed interest. But when the patient expressed a desire to be straight, the therapist showed less interest. Similarly, when the patient talked about his childhood, particularly the oedipal period, and about his feelings of being smothered by his mother and his fears of his father, the therapist was largely silent because the patient aroused feelings in himself that he had chosen to keep repressed. But when the patient talked of how he had always been attracted to men as long as he could remember, the therapist paid attention. The patient soon learned not to broach certain subjects, fearing the disapproval of the therapist (who symbolized the disapproval of the gay community, a cultural entity in its own right).

Another case involves two women, a therapist and a patient, who shared a feminist perspective. The young woman, a college student, came to the therapist complaining of a date rape that had left her shattered and unable to function. The therapist and patient quickly formed a collusion that became a resistance and counterresistance, preventing any real resolution of the woman's hysterical psychopathology. The patient had a need to see the man who had raped her as a villain and herself as completely innocent. The therapist, going along with current feminist doctrine that warns against blaming the victim, joined the patient's resistance. Even when the patient, on a few occasions, began to examine the possibility that she in some way might have provoked the rape, the therapist would quickly answer, "Stop blaming yourself."

In fact, the young women had a pattern of leading men on. Like many hysterics, she would be seductive toward a man and then, when he was alone with her and made a move, would suddenly change her mind and deny to the man that she had ever given him any messages to the contrary. The man who raped her had his own baggage of unresolved anger at women and at his mother. He was unable to countenance this seduction-and-abandonment game and, persisting in his sexual overtures, would not accept "no" for an answer.

Since this therapist's cultural counterresistance, as well as her own unresolved hysterical characterology, precluded her being able to allow the patient to explore her repetition compulsion and its underlying complexes, the patient remained stuck in this pattern of relating. The therapist did short-term crisis therapy with the patient, and soon after that the patient called her again, stating that she wanted to return for more therapy because "one of my male teachers sexually harassed me and I'm very upset."

Greenson (1967) tells of an instance in which he was analyzing an African-American man. Although the patient continually brought in dreams that indicated a great deal of mistrust and suspiciousness concerning Greenson, Greenson ignored the racial issue and interpreted these dreams as transference reactions to him derivative of early feelings about his parents. There were frequently pauses in their dialogue, and again Greenson was quick to interpret these pauses as due to a resistance to getting in touch with unconscious material. The relationship went on this way for a year, and Greenson helped the patient in problems with his career situation.

Only later did Greenson realize that he had had a counterresistance to interpreting the racial issues. He had a need—which, for the most part, was unconscious—to think of himself as liberal and hence oblivious to skin color. In the liberal culture it is considered a faux pas to acknowledge any differences between blacks and whites, and to bring up this patient's blackness seemed to be an admission of prejudice. In fact, not bringing it up was.

While at its minimal level cultural counterresistances can cause a therapist to be selectively
inattentive to certain trends, on a deeper level they
can lead to a form of indoctrination. In that case the
patient may be subject to subtle or not so subtle
intimidation and seduction. Patients in a regressed
state are quite susceptible to such an indoctrination.

This, of course, is the form of therapy most
often associated, in the past, with Russian psychiatry, and it is the theme of novels such as George
Orwell's *1984*. However, unconscious forms of
brainwashing (or, at times, not so unconscious)
may be happening in our own therapeutic community more than we think. What takes place behind
a therapist's office door is a secret between the
therapist and the patient. Those case histories that
are reported in journals and books represent only a
selected few, and even those are presented in such
a way as to illustrate a point. How do we brainwash
our patients? Let us say, for example, that a black
therapist has been raised in a cultural environment
that stressed black pride and togetherness. Suppose a black patient whose goal is to become
assimilated in the "white world" enters therapy
with this therapist. The therapist may have an
unconscious agenda for the patient: to convert him
to the cause of black togetherness. Hence, in subtle
ways, the therapist will discourage all movements
by the patient toward assimilation with whites and
encourage a kind of black separatism. He may even
suggest that the desire to assimilate with whites
represents a form of betrayal. Let us suppose,
further, that during the course of therapy the pa-

tient is regressed to a stage of infantile dependence on the therapist. In this state the therapist can literally hypnotize the patient into adopting whatever philosophy or political stance he wants. As I said, this may be happening more than we realize, and in such instances psychotherapy becomes a propaganda tool of a movement.

## LACAN'S CULTURAL COUNTERRESISTANCE

An account of Jacques Lacan's interview with a psychotic patient (Schneiderman 1980) shows how his theoretical preconceptions became a cultural counterresistance that prevented the patient from free associating and influenced him in a particular direction. Although Lacan used this interview to demonstrate his theories to other psychiatrists, it nevertheless reveals something about his way of thinking and working. In this interview, Lacan subtly communicated his psychoanalytic ideology to the patient, shaping the patient's responses. This is something that occurs in all types of psychotherapy and makes it difficult for researchers to make objective conclusions about the meanings and results of psychotherapy.

In Lacanian therapy, the therapist concentrates not on the content of what the patient says, but on signifiers—the disguised language in which the patient reveals unconscious libidinal material. The therapist uncovers the patient's signifiers and figures of speech and takes them literally, tracing them to their sources from the most recent to the most archaic. In doing so, the therapist also assumes an active, authoritarian stance, which has the effect of hastening regression, particularly in psychotic patients such as the patient in interview.

Lacan began from the outset to direct the patient. "Tell me about yourself," he ordered. When the patient remained silent, he added, "I don't know why I would not let you speak. You know very well what is happening to you" (Schneiderman 1980, p. 19). The patient then began to talk about not being able to get hold of himself, about how his thoughts and his speech seemed to come from outside himself and were not under his own control. Lacan's statement, "I don't know why I would not let you speak," sounds clever and intuitive and gets the patient started, but it also represents an intrusion into the patient's mind, which may rekindle fears of thought control by his parents.

When the patient related a repeating statement that ran through his brain, "You killed the bluebird. It's an anarchic system" (p. 20), Lacan interrupted the interview to focus on this statement. Later, when the patient used the word "osmosis" to describe how he picked up the anxiety in his household, Lacan again interrupted to explore this signifier and to tie it in with the thesis of "the real and the imaginary." Lacan was clearly not interested in helping the patient to free associate and discover for himself what was in his head. Instead, he was interested in exploring the symbolic, and he kept guiding the patient toward that goal.

This continued throughout the interview. For

example, when the patient later noted, "I tried, by poetic action, to find a balancing rhythm, a music. I was led to think that speech is the projection of an intelligence which arises toward the outside" (p. 26), Lacan tried for some time to extract from the patient more information about poetic action, speech, and intelligence. The patient, responding to this further attempt to guide him, became resistant, complaing about his anxiety about being interviewed in front of a roomful of psychiatrists. Still later Lacan and the patient became involved in an argument with respect to waking dreams and night dreams and how the patient's imposed speech fit into them. Again, Lacan was trying to decipher what the patient was signifying, focusing in particular on a statement about bluebirds wanting to kill him. The patient spoke of a paradoxical state in which he lived in a solitary circle without boundaries. Lacan argued that a circle was a boundary. The two became locked in an intellectual duel. The patient grew more and more anxious and, at the end, described how neighbors were pressuring him and had driven him to wanting to commit suicide.

In this interchange, Lacan appeared to be so wrapped up in tracing signifiers involving the imaginary and the real that he overlooked the patient's increasing anxiety and the transference meaning of what was occurring. The patient seemed to be responding to Lacan's "interrogation" by regressing more and more into psychosis. His language had become more and more symbolic and less concrete, which was what Lacan wanted in order to prove his theory.

Lacan's need to prove his theory served as a counterresistance that prevented the natural evolution of the interview. Another therapist might have explored the transference relationship, focusing on the patient's projections that his neighbors, the psychiatrists in the audience, and even the therapist, were out to get him. By doing so, the therapist could help the patient integrate his fragmented psyche, taking back split-off parts and becoming aware of his own anger. Lacan, however, is not particularly interested in the patient's feelings, but in his language.

In the end of the interview, Lacan concludes by predicting that the patient will sooner or later commit suicide. This prediction is more a reflection of the bias of Lacan's ideological stance than of the actual predicament of the patient. Indeed, one could make any of a number of conclusions from what the patient said during this interview. Making hasty and arbitrary conclusions or predictions about a patient is one of the most common ways of derailing a therapy. It is a resistance to allowing things to evolve naturally.

## CULTURAL COUNTERRESISTANCES IN TRAINING

The therapy environment is a microcosm of the cultural environment, and all of the cultural strife in society comes into focus in the therapy dyad. The same clashes of religion, ideology, race, gender, sexual orientation, and class that take place in society also happen in the therapy office, and the sudden shifts in cultural values brought about by economic depression, war, or zealous movements trickle down into the therapy milieu. It is no easier to resolve these clashes and confluences in the therapy office than it is in society in general, and many topics remain as sacred cows that both the therapist and the patient avoid.

The confusion and clash of cultural biases affect therapy training and literature as well. I am a graduate of two psychotherapy institutes and attended a third for two years, and I seldom heard instructors, supervisors, or training analysts mention cultural counterresistances. People knew about them, but they were not the things that were emphasized in training. In two of the institutes there was a tacit—and sometimes not so tacit—allegiance to liberal cultural values, and to suggest that such cultural values might be counterresistances in therapy would have been tantamount to heresy. On the contrary, everybody was pressured to conform to them. In the third, conservative, authoritarian values persisted.

Ironically, cultural bias is often built into psychotherapy training institutes. Each institute or school of psychoanalysis and psychotherapy has its own bias that attracts particular candidates. Traditional psychoanalytic institutes draw candidates who embrace a traditional point of view; radical institutes draw candidates who embrace a radical point of view; religious institutes draw candidates who embrace a religious point of view. Each school thus becomes a center for the transmission of its particular ideology, and each encourages a particular kind of cultural counterresistance. (For more on this topic, see Chapter 7.)

Psychoanalytic and psychotherapeutic literature also reflects the clash of cultural values. For example, Freud and his views have come under attack from many groups whose values clash with those of classical psychoanalysis. Kanefield (1985), writing in the *Journal of the American Academy of Psychoanalysis*, typifies the feminist attack, debunking Freud's concepts of female development, asserting that "Freud's view of women as castrated men, reconciled to inferiority due to their biological lack, is misogynous." She goes on to criticize what she sees as Freud's presumption that "women are lesser because they are different than men," calling it "deeply sexist and unfounded." She concludes: "The fact remains that patriarchal society has devalued women's bodies, minds and contributions, and that women themselves have learned to disqualify their own experiences" (p. 352).

This kind of writing represents an acting out of a cultural resistance through the written word. That a cultural resistance is being acted out is obvious by the tone and type of argumentation used. The writer does not offer quotes from Freud to back up her argument, nor does she attempt to refute his supposed contentions through reason. Instead, she refutes him through character assassination; he is misogynous and sexist. Nor are her conclusions about how patriarchal society has "devalued women's bodies, minds and contributions" based on any scientific finding or reasonable debate, but rather on a consensus of feminists and their supporters, repeated again and again, here and elsewhere, like a church litany.

Changing cultural values are also reflected in the literature with regard to trends in therapy. In the 1960s and 1970s in the United States there was the so-called sexual revolution, and during this time therapists wrote about such things as nude marathons and advocated using drugs like marijuana and LSD in therapy. One psychiatrist, Martin Shepard (1972) thought that there was nothing particularly wrong about a therapist having sex with a patient, and he even believed it might be beneficial at times. "While I think that most therapists are far too ambivalent, guilty, dishonest, or exploitative to be able helpfully and healthily to fuck a patient, I do not believe that any form of interaction can or ought to be banned or ballyhooed in and of itself" (p. 154). In the 1980s, values with regard to sexuality went to perhaps the opposite extreme (a backlash). AIDS reared its head and charges of sexual abuse and harassment filled the air and airwaves. Any therapist who advocated sex with a patient, nude marathons, or the use of drugs, was hastily chastised, stigmatized, and "defrocked."

Ideally, therapists need to be able to transcend considerations of religion, ideology, politics, race, gender, ethnicity, regionalism, class, and sexual orientation. They should also be above the shifting tide of values and the ever-present social pressures to adopt succeeding values as the "ultimate true way," which has gone on throughout history. To the extent that they can be, they will succeed at their jobs of helping people become themselves. If not, they will help people to remain attached to a religion or ideology, merged symbiotically with a group that becomes a substitute and enabling caretaker, that prevents them from growing toward complete independence.

From the beginning of his founding of psychoanalysis, Freud tried to keep it independent of government, academia, and religion, knowing that cultural factors would corrupt its highly touted neutrality. He had the right idea, I think, but unfortunately he is no longer around.

**7**

---

# Counterresistance in Three Schools of Therapy

Each school of psychoanalysis and psychotherapy not only has its own particular therapeutic orientation, but also its own particular attitude with respect to doing therapy. This attitude brings along with it a particular way of relating to the patient and a particular way of counterresisting.

I have narrowed this phenomenon down to three schools that represent three general orientations: the classical psychoanalytic model as formulated by Freud, with its passive mode of doing therapy; the self psychology model as formulated by Heinz Kohut (but which harks back to Jung), with its spiritual mode of doing therapy; and the modern psychoanalytic model as formulated by Hyman Spotnitz (which leads back to Wilhelm Reich), with its active mode of doing therapy.

One reason why each school has its own peculiar counterresistance tendencies has to do with the kinds of people who are attracted to it. Each of the three schools of psychoanalysis under consideration draws its own particular kinds of followers, depending on the leader of that school and its philosophy. Self psychology, it seems to me, appeals especially to those who want to deny their aggression, and the most prevalent kind of countertransference problem among self psychologists involves a subjective twinship countertransference (Kohut 1971) in which the analyst joins the patient's narcissistic tendency to grandiose thinking and the denial of rage. Classical analysis appeals to obsessive-compulsive and passive–aggressive types, like Freud, and their countertransference dilemmas tend to be connected with a stubborn rigidity to the blank screen and to institutionalized passive aggression. Modern analysis, in my view, attracts people who, like Spotnitz, are mavericks, and who believe in getting aggression out in the open. Their countertransference problems revolve around subjective, often self-indulgent, uses of confrontation and aggression.

There is a famous psychological experiment that may shed further light on countertransference difficulties in relation to an institution, such as a school of psychoanalysis, and to the leader of such a school: Milgram's (1974) research study on obedience to authority. In his experiment he asked people to help him with a study of how punishment affects learning. Participants were asked to administer electric shocks to "learners" who sat behind screens, strapped to a chair, with electrodes attached to their arms. The participants were told that the straps were used to prevent excessive movement during the experiment, and that although electric shocks would cause pain, they would not cause any permanent tissue damage. The participants were then led through the experiment by experimenters (authority figures), who instructed the participants to press levers that were labeled from 15 to 450 volts. The participants could see the learners' faces behind the screen contorted with pain and hear their screams of agony as they pressed the levers. However, most participants, men and women and from all walks of life, kept pressing the levers and ignored the pain of the learners (who were actually actors).

This experiment demonstrated a certain obedience to authority that seems to be present in a great many people, but it does not explain why it exists. My interpretation is that it has to do with the general narcissism and aggression that is part of the human condition, and with the need to believe in an authority greater than oneself, who gives one permission to act out that narcissism and aggression. The authority permits one to regress to a state of dependency and absolution of responsibility, a state in which one can feel grandiose and superior (it's not me getting punished, it's him, because I'm luckier and superior), and can act out aggression in good conscience (for the good of science).

The leaders of the various schools of therapy serve this function to some degree, modeling a certain way of expressing narcissism and aggression, be it passive-aggression, denial of aggression, or sadistic aggression. In this sense, each leader and each school become unofficial sponsors of institutionalized counterresistance. This is not to say that these schools set out to do this or that this is the main thing that they do; rather, it is an unconscious by-product of what they do. Each school has it's own typical countransference as well as counterresistance.

Most schools revolve around a cultlike figure. Freud and the world of classical analysis have often been described as a cult, as have both the self psychology and modern psychoanalytic movements. Each is a self-sustaining world with its own value system, backed up by unofficial mass consensus. At the center of these systems are the institutes, with their monasterylike atmospheres, their training analysts (high priests), and their supervision groups. Each system perpetuates its particular way of relating.

Greenson (1978), commenting on this topic, notes "Differences in attitude toward adversity, the ability to endure uncertainty, to take risks, the quality of their libidinal and aggressive strivings, the ability to stand alone, all play a part in the formation of schools of psychoanalysis" (p. 350). He goes on to say that all schools become parochial and insular and follow the dictates of an "ideal analyst" or the belief in a "perfect system": "If I imagine an analytic session with a 'true believer' analyst repeating the catechism of his school, it is hard to see this as a living creative experience for either the patient or the therapist" (p. 354). In a sense, I am attempting an elaboration of Greenson's observations, tracking down the kind of countertransference and counterresistance typical of each school. (See Table 7–1).

**Table 7–1.**  Counterresistance in Three Schools of Therapy

| School | Original Model | What is Resisted | Typical Counter-transference | Typical Counter-resistance |
|---|---|---|---|---|
| Classical Analysis (passive) | Sigmund Freud | Confrontation, disorder, tenderness, craziness | Passive-avoidant counter-transference | Passive-aggressive frustration of patient |
| Self Psychology (spiritual) | Carl Jung | Aggression, separation, devaluation, annihilation, reengulfment | Twinship counter-transference | Grandiose (spiritual) alliance with patient |
| Modern Analysis (active) | Wilhelm Reich | Anxiety, domination, manipulation, degradation | Authoritarian counter-transference | Domination (taming) of patient |

## COUNTERRESISTANCE IN CLASSICAL PSYCHOANALYSIS (KOHUT AND MR. Z.)

Kohut (1979), in his description of his first analysis of Mr. Z., provides us with an excellent example of a typical counterresistance of the classical psychoanalytic variety. Mr. Z., a tall, intellectual graduate student, came to Kohut when he was still practicing what he described as classical analysis. The analysis revealed that Mr. Z. was a lonely man who still lived with his mother. In his fantasies Mr. Z. abjectly performed menial tasks for a domineering woman, who forced him to perform the sexual act. At the moment of ejaculation, he would feel like a horse straining under a coachman's whip. He recounted a lonely childhood as an only child, which was interrupted when he was about 3½ years old, when his father became ill and had to stay in the hospital for several months. There the father fell in love with a nurse and proceeded to move in with her. The affair lasted about 18 months, and his father returned when Mr. Z. was 5 years-old. Family life was not the same after his father returned. While his father was away, the child had grown used to having his mother to himself and slept in his father's twin bed. When his father returned, he slept in the same room and heard and witnessed his parents loudly and, it seemed, violently, making love.

Kohut describes Mr. Z.'s transference in the first year as "a regressive mother transference." He saw the patient as an unrealistic, grandiose person who demanded complete control of the analytic situation and expected Kohut to admire and dote on him as his mother had done, particularly while his father was away. Kohut intervened by giving him repeated "reconstructive interpretations" of his behavior. He would explain how Mr. Z. had transferred his mother onto him, how he expected special treatment from him, and how this need for special treatment could be traced back to this time when he had his mother to himself.

"He blew up in rages against me, time after time," Kohut writes. "Indeed the picture he presented during the first year and a half of the analysis was dominated by his rage" (p. 5). Mr. Z. would rage about Kohut's interpretations, scheduling difficulties, vacations, and other matters. "You don't understand me!" he kept complaining.

Kohut would calmly counter with yet another interpretation.

After a year and a half, Kohut recalls, the patient became abruptly calmer and less demanding. Kohut assumed this was because his interpretations had been successful, but the patient disagreed, saying, "The change has taken place not primarily because of a change in me, but because of something *you* did. Remember when you began one of your interpretations about my insatiable narcissistic demands with the phrase, 'Of course, it hurts when one is not given what one assumes to be one's due'? That's what did it" (p. 5). Kohut did not take this comment seriously at the time, but thought the patient was again resisting by denying the effectiveness of his interpretations.

As the analysis proceeded Kohut focused, as he had been taught to do at the Chicago Psychoanalytic Institute, on the Oedipus complex, the castration complex, childhood libidinal strivings, and the primal scene. At the same time, he ignored pregenital material. He described this first analysis as "fully in tune with the classical theories of psychoanalysis" (p. 7). He interpreted Mr. Z.'s masochism as sexualization of his guilt about the preoedipal possession of his mother and rejection of his father. He further interpreted that Mr. Z. had to create the imagery of a domineering phallic woman to assuage his castration anxiety. This imagery was designed to deny the existence of human beings who had no penises, by giving women power over his sexuality.

The analysis lasted about four years. Gradually, Mr. Z. seemed to improve. His masochistic preoccupations diminished and he moved out of his mother's house and began dating a woman a year older than he. Toward the end of the analysis, Mr. Z. brought in a dream that Kohut again interpreted according to classical psychoanalytic teaching. Mr. Z. dreamed that he was in a house, standing at a door that was open just a crack. Outside was his father, his arms full of gifts, wanting to enter the door. Mr. Z. was terrified and tried to close the door in order to keep the father out. Kohut interpreted that this dream referred to the boy's ambivalent attitude toward the returning father, his castration fear, his fear of male competition, his incestuous tie to his mother, and to his passive-homosexual attitude to his father.

As the termination phase wore down, Kohut thought something was not quite right; the entire phase was "emotionally shallow and unexciting" (p. 9), but he let it go. The patient and therapist parted with a friendly handshake. Four and a half years later the patient returned for four more years of analysis. By this time Kohut had developed his theory of self psychology and had stopped doing classical analysis.

He now realized that in his first analysis he had not given the patient the responses he needed—he had, in other words, acted out an institutionally sponsored, *classical analytic counterresistance* (these are my words, not his). He had treated the patient according to how he had been taught in his institute.

At the beginning of the second analysis, as in the first, Mr. Z. idealized Kohut. While in the first analysis Kohut had immediately interpreted this idealization; in the second he did not, and after two weeks the idealization faded of its own accord, replaced by another transference in which Mr. Z. became "self-centered, demanding, insisting on perfect empathy, and inclined to react with rage at the slightest out-of-tuneness with his psychological states, with the slightest misunderstanding of his communications" (pp. 11–12). While in the first analysis Kohut had looked upon this behavior as defensive, tolerated it as unavoidable, and confronted it with interpretations, in the second analysis he saw it as an analytically valuable replica of traumatic childhood material being revived in the transference.

In addition, during the first analysis he had a need to help the patient relinquish his narcissistic demands and grow up—he had an agenda for the patient. His view of his relationship with the patient's mother also differed from the first to the second analysis. In the first, he focused on the mother's incestuous tie to the son, while in the second the actual character of the mother came more sharply into focus. This rigid focus on the incestuous tie was probably felt by the patient as criticism and as a suggestion that he separate from his mother. It did not help him to work through his feelings about her.

Although Kohut presents the first analysis as classical psychoanalysis and the second as self psychology, critics contend that the first was simply bad classical analysis while the second was good classical analysis. Meyerson (1981), for example, notes that in the second analysis Kohut gave Mr. Z. the sense that it was all right for him to have negative feelings about his mother and to express his rage, masochism, and exhibitionism, while in the first he discouraged him. Through his strict adherence to neutrality, the blank screen, and abstinence, and through his ego-dystonic interpretations, he put the patient into a double bind. If Mr. Z. continued to behave in a demanding, grandiose, rageful manner, he would meet with disapproval, but if he did not he would have to pretend to be somebody else in order to get approval.

In the beginning of the analysis, Kohut could not tolerate being idealized by Mr. Z. and immediately interpreted this idealization. This is a counterresistance that points to a defense against the therapist's own grandiosity. Similarly, his inability to tolerate Mr. Z.'s demandingness, his apparent rush to interpret it, and his rage reactions indicated that the therapist had not worked through and integrated his own feelings of entitlement and rage. Apparently there was a projection, and perhaps a projective identification. The patient became the possessor of the disowned aspects of the therapist, that is, those feelings and impulses that the therapist found distasteful, and they then had to be expunged from the patient.

Searles (1979) highlighted this aspect of classical psychoanalytic counterresistance in alluding to an unconscious desire to drive the patient crazy, which linked it to the defense mechanism of reaction formation and "a desire to externalize, and thus get rid of, the threatening craziness in oneself" (p. 265). Kohut and Mr. Z. had many similarities; both were only children, both lost their fathers at an early age, both had lived with their mothers, and both were large men with timid personalities (timidity being a defense against grandiosity). While Kohut's interpretations were consciously meant to diminish Mr. Z.'s grandiosity and rage, unconsciously he may have wanted to make the patient even crazier, to externalize and get rid of the craziness in himself and to feel superior to the patient.

A telltale sign of Kohut's subjective counterresistance was his labeling of Mr. Z. as having "a regressive mother transference." Regression is an aspect of all transferences; hence, his using this word is perhaps a kind of psychoanalytic overkill that points to his own negativity at the time.

To be sure, any approach to therapy can be done well or poorly, and a good classical analyst would not be prone to the kind of counterresistance demonstrated by this case history. What Kohut was pointing out, and what I am reiterating, are the pitfalls of this particular model of therapy. These pitfalls center around a passive-avoidant countertransference, a passive-aggressive frustration of the patient, and a general resistance to confrontation and to the craziness and perversity of pre-oedipal material. It was precisely this kind of counterresistance that sabotaged Kohut's first analysis with Mr. Z.

Incidentally, this case is also reminiscent of Freud's four-year treatment of the Wolf Man, which also appeared to end successfully. In this case, Freud wished to avoid the Wolf's Man's craziness. Like Mr. Z., the Wolf Man needed another analysis later on.

## COUNTERRESISTANCE IN SELF
## PSYCHOLOGY

Just as Kohut took note of the hazards of the classical approach, so others have critized his self psychology approach to therapy. Kohut's writing is replete with complex discussions of the patient's need for a selfobject, for transmuting internalizations, and for narcissistic transference, that is, idealizing or twinship, with the therapist. What he did not write about is the therapist's corresponding need to make the patient a selfobject, to use the patient for transmuting internalizations, and to form an idealizing or twinship countertransference with the patient. His discussion of countertransference was minimal and was primarily concerned with the problem of the analyst who "feels oppressed by his own narcissistic tensions [and] attempts to fend off the patient's overt idealization" (1971, p. 164).

Most self psychologists, like most therapists in general, are competent professionals. However, when they err, they tend to err in certain ways typical of them. While classical analysts passive-aggressively frustrate patients, self psychologists form grandiose alliances with them and deny their own, and their patients' aggression. Their idealizing and twinship transference–countertransference dyads at times become collusions of grandeur. Self psychology, like Jungian psychoanalysis, attracts therapists with a narcissistic character structure, so that the patient comes to be a selfobject for them, reflecting their spiritual goodness, validating that they are warm, empathic people. They have unresolved needs for symbiotic merger, and the holding environment they provide becomes a means for returning to this state of symbiosis, which then results in what Searles (1979) has referred to as symbiotic clinging. This keeps a patient stuck in a pregenital stage of development.

One self psychologist, a young woman, had a mother who had devalued her. This mother was a critical, perfectionistic woman who had targeted her oldest daughter as the recipient of her split-off projected self. The mother gave her daughter the message that she was bad and unlovable. As a consequence, the oldest daughter enlisted her younger sister as a selfobject. She became the surrogate mother to this younger sister and trained her to give her the message that she was good and lovable.

When she grew up, she was attracted to self psychology because it seemed to stress being empathic and supportive—that is, being good and lovable. Through the arena of psychotherapy, she could repeatedly prove her goodness by being good and loving to her patients. She induced her patients into becoming selfobjects for her, just as she had done with her sister. Her patients, many of whom were younger women, would revere her for her kindness and nobility, and she in turn would be the adored figure who would accept and approve of them. However, both patient and therapist would unconsciously resist anything that smacked of criticism or aggression; hence real relating and real progress were stifled. Her patients either stayed with her for years in a dependent relationship or "got better" and maintained sisterly correspondences with her.

On occasion an errant self psychological approach can hasten disaster. I recently learned of a case involving a young male attorney with strong paranoid features and an older male therapist who had written papers on self psychology. The patient had sought out the therapist after reading one of his papers and hoped to enlist him as a selfobject. He was a bright, slightly effeminate young man who had been an only child and whose parents had virtually kept him prisoner in his bedroom during the first three years of his life and told him that he was "unfit for company." They made him feel that his thoughts, feelings, and perceptions were crazy.

"I'm not crazy," was one of the first things he said to the therapist when he entered his office. This was a theme that repeated itself throughout the therapy. He would insist that he was not crazy, then look at the door and ask if anybody could overhear their conversation. He made the therapist swear again and again that he would never divulge anything he said to anybody, especially not to the corporation where he worked, because they were currently investigating him and he was in danger of being fired. He said he did not want the therapist to use his real name on his records. Toward the end of the first session, when the therapist began to write down the patient's name, the patient leaned forward and snapped, "Don't do that."

"Don't do what?" the therapist replied.

"Don't write my name in your book."

"How am I going to make another appointment?"

"I'll tell you in a minute. I'll tell you what to write. But first let me explain something. I'm not crazy. When you truly understand my situation you'll see what I mean. I'm just under a lot of stress right now and I have to be careful."

"What name would you like me to put down in my appointment book?"

"All right. All right. I'll tell you. Write down—you're going to think this is crazy, but it does have a meaning—write down the initials 'N.S.' That's right, N.S. Write it down. Do you know what it means? Would you like me to tell you what it means?"

"Okay."

"It means 'Now Seer.' It's my pseudonym. I write poems. I didn't mention that I write poems, did I? I'm a poet as well as an attorney. And when I publish my poems, I sign them 'N.S.'"

During the course of the next eight months the therapist saw N.S. five times a week. He felt frightened and overwhelmed by the patient from the beginning and struggled against (rather than accepting and analyzing) these feelings. When a therapist, or anybody, struggles against feelings, the feelings become stronger. N.S. kept insisting almost every day that he was not paranoid and that he was, instead, a seer who saw things others were simply not wise enough to see. Whatever problems he had were caused by other people's victimization of him. He had had numerous therapists, and he complained that all of them had oppressed him by labeling him, telling him that he was paranoid and needed therapy. The self psychologist did not label him—at least not in the beginning. Instead, he became his "selfobject"—allowing the patient to idealize him and tolerating his demandingness, mirroring him the way he wanted to be mirrored.

Like the queen in the children's story, *Snow White*, he demanded that his mirror tell him he was not only the fairest, but also the smartest and healthiest, and that in fact the rest of the world, particularly those psychotherapists who had dared to label him, were "full of shit."

The therapist not only went along with everything, but also formed a twinship countertransference, which resulted in a twinship counterresistance. He went along with the patient's delusion that the two of them were the only two sane people in the world. As their relationship progressed, N.S. began to demand more and more. If they were indeed intellectual twins, why should they not write an article together? Why not a book? A book, say, about the psychological and legal ramifications of mental illness. Indeed, why should N.S. pay the therapist if they were actually on the same level? Why should they not simply become colleagues and join forces against the corruption of the world? To all this the therapist gave tacit agreement, nodding his head.

The therapist was in actuality a competent and astute person, but this patient aroused strong countertransference feelings. He was like a hurricane blowing through his door. The therapist could feel the tension, the pent up rage, the anxiety in his every word and movement. He could feel himself tensing up as the patient spoke in a manic, rambling voice, not allowing the therapist to get a word in during the course of the session, but at the end of the sessions insisting that the therapist, on his own time, tell him what he thought.

"Time's up," the therapist would say.

"You're not going to just leave me like this. Oh, please, please, don't do that to me."

"But—"

"No, no, no. Please, please, you've got to tell me. I can't leave here if you don't tell me!"

He found himself constantly enraged, frightened, and rendered impotent psychologically by N.S.'s extremely controlling behavior. Unable to analyze and resolve these overwhelming feelings, he attempted to deal with them by smiling and nodding and being a good selfobject. He thought that by being everything the patient wanted of him, by not labeling him as other therapists had done, he might eventually be able to forge an alliance that would strengthen the patient's ego so that he could hear the truth.

As the days passed the patient became increasingly adamant about being the therapist's colleague and writing a book with him. The therapist kept saying, "Not yet, let's keep going. We're making good progress." Suddenly the patient called the therapist and said, "I'm quitting therapy. I don't need therapy. I'm not crazy, and you and I both know it. Now, when can we meet for coffee and discuss our book?"

The therapist refused to write an article or book with him, declined to accept him as a colleague, and insisted instead that N.S. come back to complete his therapy. This made N.S. see the therapist as a betrayer and as another therapist trying to oppress him, which sent him into a paranoid panic state. Subsequently he began acting out at the corporation where he worked, furiously demanding that his supervisors and fellow employees become selfobjects and that they mirror him as the fairest lawyer in the land. When they scoffed, he became spiteful and outrageous, so that administrators called in a psychiatrist and had him committed to a mental hospital. He was found mentally unstable and soon lost his license to practice. His wife left him and friends abandoned him. He was shattered.

This is a case in which the mirror lied as long as it could, but eventually it could not lie anymore. The queen was catapulted into harsh reality. Following what he thought were the tenets of self psychology, the therapist had attempted to be empathic and to provide a holding environment for N.S. However, unwittingly, due to his own characterological counterresistance, he was setting him up for a great fall.

Spotnitz noted the difficulties of handling the feelings that a schizophrenic patient arouses. "In my experience, the main source of countertransference resistance in the relationship with a schizophrenic patient is the therapist's need to defend himself against the rage and anxiety induced by the patient's hostile impulses" (1985, p. 242). He explains that many therapists particularly have a need to deny their murderous feelings. Searles (1979) has made the same point.

The relentless assault of a patient such as N.S. would try any therapist. Under such an assault, one either puts one's foot down immediately and confronts the patient immediately, or one joins the flow of the storm and gets caught in the wind. Once you get caught in the wind, you are helpless until the wind dies down, and then you may not have enough strength to say anything.

The therapist had a characterological counter-resistance that manifested itself in a denial of the murderous rage inside him and a denial that the patient was infuriating. So instead of confronting him, the therapist appeased him. He tried to emphasize the positive while denying the negative. He was not aware of appeasing him, but thought that he was providing a holding environment. He had been drawn into a symbiotic twinship counter-transference with the patient in which he defended against fears of separation (from the primitive mother) as well as from fears of annihilation and reengulfment. Eventually his appeasing behavior led to increasingly more outrageous demands.

## COUNTERRESISTANCE IN MODERN PSYCHOANALYSIS

Modern psychoanalysis, a school of psychoanalysis that was founded in the 1960s by Spotnitz, follows the model established by Reich. It is noted for its emphasis on aggression and for the treatment of more disturbed personalities. Central to modern psychoanalytic treatment theory is emotional communication with the patient, confrontation of the patient's aggression, and, at times, the use of the "toxic response," which is roughly equivalent to giving the patient back some of his own "medicine."

Writing about the toxic response, Spotnitz

(1976) warns that "the very fact that the emotional quality of the transference reactions is thereby intensified introduces the possibility of a new source of error: contamination of the analytic situation by an incorrect confrontation" (p. 56). Spotnitz concludes: "Countertransference cannot be used with complete confidence unless it has been purged of its subjective elements" (p. 57). In other words, the main way modern analysts counterresist is by expressing subjective aggression.

A modern analyst had a borderline, suicidal patient whose roommate was also borderline and suicidal. The patient came to him one day and asked him if he could refer her roommate to an analyst who worked in a similar way. The analyst said he could, and referred the roommate to another modern analyst in his supervision group. His patient had given him permission to fill in the other analyst of the roommate's background, so he did so. He told the other analyst that his patient's roommate, a young woman in her early twenties, had a history of suicidal attempts and had recently been in Bellevue Hospital for a month. He also told her that the two roommates had taken a wild car trip across the United States the previous summer, in which they had reveled in seducing and teasing men and feeling superior to them. He said she had been to several therapists and had not liked any of them.

The second therapist took the referral with reluctance, confessing that she felt terrified of working with suicides. The first therapist replied in a way typical of modern analysts: "You're having all the right feelings." The second analyst, a woman who had recently completed training, felt reassured.

After her initial session with this patient, the second analyst presented the case to the supervision group. Her tone and manner as she presented it was not that of somebody seeking help, but more of someone seeking confirmation of a job well done. Her presentation was delivered in a deadpan style that garnered many laughs. She had confronted the patient, she said, from the moment she walked into her office. When the patient spoke in a quiet, timid way, the therapist demanded that she speak up. When she fell silent the therapist warned her that if she wanted to be in therapy with her she would have to talk. At one point the therapist said, "I heard that you've already rejected numerous therapists, so I suppose you'll be looking for reasons to reject me." At another point she said, "I know all about how you went on that trip with your girlfriend across the United States and how the two of you think you're superior to all men, and if you think you're going to be superior to me and pull that teasing, withholding nonsense on me, you're quite mistaken." She warned her, furthermore, that she would not tolerate any suicidal behavior and that she would not work with her at all if she did not have a consultation with a psychiatrist immediately and get put on medication. "I don't want you committing suicide on me," she told her. "I'm not going to let you ruin my reputation with any of your spiteful suicidal manipulations." When the patient began to mumble again, she said, "And stop that mumbling. I won't have you torturing me with that mumbling either." She went on like this for the entire session, and the patient eventually burst into tears and left.

Most of the supervision group, as well as the leader, expressed admiration for her work. "You did a great job," somebody said. They saw her as having stood up to the patient's unconscious murderous intentions from the start, of having used the feelings the patient was inducing to good effect, and of preempting her attempts to manipulate through suicide and withholding. Only one colleague tried to say something slightly critical, and as soon as he did so the presenter responded with, "No, that's way off base," and the colleague quickly backed down. In fact, this analyst did not wish to receive any criticism of her work—her own narcissistic grandiosity prevented it—so she encouraged only positive feedback and discouraged negative feedback. She had a need to always be seen as good, noble, right, and nearly perfect.

While I agree that it is necessary to confront suicidal patients, there was something excessive about the way this analyst confronted this patient. No attempt was made in the group to explore the analyst's feelings in terms of how they may have been connected to events in her own past, but I happened to know that she had had an extremely rivalrous relationship with a younger sister who would cry and complain bitterly to her parents that the analyst was torturing her. It seemed to me that the terror that the analyst felt toward this patient, before she even met her, had to do with these unresolved feelings from the past. She had, in effect, acted out these feelings of terror by assaulting the patient with insults. It was a compulsive acting out, not something she had planned after discussing her feelings with a supervisor and coming to grips with them. She seemed to have a need to vomit up all the terror she couldn't tolerate, to insult and degrade this patient and intimidate her into submission, perhaps as she had done with her younger sister. Afterwards, she and the group rationalized that this assault was a modern analytic intervention.

In hypnosis, incidentally, there is a method of induction that relies on shock and intimidation. It is sometimes also used by terrorists, and has been called "the Patty Hearst Syndrome,"—after the heiress who was captured by terrorists, fell in love with one of her captors, came to believe in their cause, and even robbed a bank for them. Shock and intimidation can send somebody into a hypnotic trance, a regression in which he or she then becomes open to the intimidator's every command—at least for a while. I had the feeling that this analyst, in acting out subjective countertransference in this manner, had in essence hypnotized her patient and shocked her into a temporary submission.

For a few months she did as she was told. The analyst reported that she had a psychiatric consultation and received medication. She came to her sessions on time and paid on time. She talked loudly enough for the analyst to hear and listened to the analyst's comments. However, after several weeks she stopped taking her medication and went into a tailspin. When she told the analyst she had stopped taking the medication, the therapist re-

plied, "In that case we'll have to stop the therapy."
When she complained, the therapist rebuked her in
an "I told you so" tone of self-righteous disgust that
suggested that the patient was incorrigibly bad.
(This tone came across as she reported on the session during group supervision.) The patient went
home to the Midwest, had a breakdown, and her
parents admitted her to a mental hospital. The analyst expressed relief to the supervision group at
ridding herself of a burden, adding that she was glad
that she had protected herself from any legal responsibility by referring her to a psychiatrist.

This case raises questions about the culture of
modern analysis. I have occasionally observed a
sarcastic attitude toward patients in modern analytic conferences. This can be a healthy thing,
allowing analysts to be honest about their negative
feelings and let off steam among one another, as
long as it is done in that light. However, the danger
is that sarcasm may override objectivity. In the
above-mentioned case, did the analyst's deadpan,
ridiculing manner contribute to the group's over-
looking the signs of subjective countertransference
and counterresistance?

Another case involves an analyst who, perhaps
because he was an experienced analyst, thought
that he could break a couple of the fundamental
rules of modern analysis.

The patient was a young woman, an analytic
trainee, who had seen the analyst when he appeared on a panel at a conference and had ap-
proached him afterwards to express an interest in
learning about modern analysis. The patient
quickly joined one of the analyst's supervision

groups and then began seeing the analyst as a therapy patient.

On about the third session of therapy, as the patient was lying on the couch with her legs slightly spread apart, the analyst asked, "Mrs. A., why are you lying with your legs spread out? Did you want me to come over and stick my hand under your skirt?" "I should say not," the horrified patient replied.

The analyst had diagnosed the patient as a masochistic personality who, like most masochistic personality types, was an injustice collector. Also, like most masochists, she was also provocative—inducing punishment from others through a self-deprecating humor, a sulky expression, and a penchant for delivering interpretations of other people's behavior toward her including the senior analyst's. The analyst felt provoked by the patient from the beginning and seduced by her sulky attitude. Therefore, he decided to confront the patient at the outset by giving her the responses she was provoking.

However, the timing and appropriateness of these interventions were questionable. The rule in modern psychoanalysis—as well as in psychoanalysis in general—is to refrain from characterological interpretations, much less ego-dystonic confrontations until a firm therapeutic alliance has been established. This is particularly true in working with narcissistic patients and also with most neurotics. An exception would be an acting-out borderline, who would need to be confronted right off, but in the proper way. This patient was a neurotic with narcissistic features, and she felt verbally raped by the sexual remark. She perceived it as a sadistic attack that confirmed her masochistic fantasies and re-created feelings of fear she harbored about her own father. Rather than advance therapeutic progress, this remark impeded it (the patient clammed up and missed subsequent sessions).

Why did an experienced senior analyst break the rules and make such interventions? He thought he was doing it to confront the patient's provocations and seductiveness. However, it seems likely that he was also aroused by subjective sadistic impulses stemming from unresolved sadomasochistic relations in his past. It may also be that his own phallic-narcissistic feelings had become excited by the patient. Perhaps he felt intimidated by her beauty and intelligence. At any rate, the fact that the intervention harmed rather than helped the therapy relationship indicates that he was somehow characterologically susceptible to the patient's provocations.

Later on this same analyst began to break another rule of modern analysis, the rule about getting the patient to say everything. The patient would come in and begin venting her feelings about something and the analyst would suddenly interrupt her, saying, "Could you lower your voice?" The patient would ask why, and the analyst would say, "I get the impression this is what you've always done, ranted and raved about everybody. Does it help? I think you need to do less ranting and raving and more analyzing." Again the patient felt attacked and degraded by the analyst and clammed up. "You're supposed to say everything that comes into your head," the analyst pressed on. The patient remained silent, feeling caught up in a no-win situation. If she said everything that came into her head, she would probably end up ranting and raving. But if she ranted and raved the analyst would tell her to shut up. The result was that an impasse developed that lasted for the duration of the therapy, eventually leading to its premature termination.

The question arises again: why did the analyst, who should have known better, break this rule? In his own mind he believed he was using the feelings induced by the patient to devise this therapeutic approach. He had begun to see the patient as not only provocative but also menacing, as trying to use her vindictiveness to intimidate him into giving her what she wanted. Therefore, he decided to respond to this vindictiveness by trying to shut it down. However, by shutting it down, the analyst prevented this aspect of the patient's behavior from erupting full-blown in the transference, blocking any chance to analyze it in a meaningful way.

At this point it appeared that the analyst was reacting not only to subjective sadistic impulses, but also to feelings of envy and paranoia. The patient was quite verbal and quite gifted and had been called upon to give a half-dozen presentations at psychoanalytic conferences during the time she was training with the senior analyst and had, in fact, in some ways surpassed the analyst in stature. More and more she had begun to analyze the analyst with interpretations like, "You've projectively identified me as a bad patient and are persecuting me." All this may have aroused feelings of envy as well as sibling rivalry (the analyst had an

older sister who had tormented him as a child).
Possibly the senior analyst also felt unconscious
guilt about the sadism he had directed at the
patient, and had become paranoid about the possibility of a counterattack by the patient, whose
intellect could be sharp and cutting. All these
things combined might have caused him to want to
shut the patient down. In essence the analyst got
drawn into a sadomasochistic struggle with the
patient and was unable to analyze himself or the
patient. In time this led to the patient's leaving
therapy.

The third example involves a woman analyst
and a younger male patient. The patient was in
both group and individual therapy with the woman
analyst. From the outset the analyst found herself
feeling uncomfortable whenever the man spoke of
his sexual exploits with women. He was a passive-
aggressive man who could not commit to a woman
and who tended to find fault with them and leave
them soon after he had had sex with them. The
analyst began to feel morally outraged by the
man's treatment of women and therefore she could
not empathize with him or appreciate the cruelty
that he had suffered at the hands of a depressed
mother and hostile father in his early childhood.
This moral outrage stemmed both from her own
unresolved castration complex and from the current cultural climate in America that reinforced
women's feelings of moral outrage toward men.
This, in turn, led to a counterresistance.

As a result of these subjective feelings, she
could not tolerate his talk about relationships with
women. When he used terms like "sleazebag" or

"bimbo" to describe women he had sexually con-
quered and dumped, she felt enraged. She decided
that this rage had been entirely induced by him,
and that he was in fact deliberately trying to degrade and annoy her and other women in the
group; therefore she determined to give him back a
"treated dose" of the toxic emotions he was inducing in her. The next time he began talking
about "sleazebags" and "bimbos" in the group she
was ready.

"And how about you?" she asked. "What kind
of bag are you?"

The other members of the group laughed.

"What do you mean?"

"Are you a sleazebag or a scumbag or a barf-
bag?"

"I don't know what you're getting at."

"Well, if you go out with all these bags, then
you must be one yourself, don't you think so?"

"Why are you saying this?"

"Why do you think?"

"You're not supposed to judge me. A therapist
isn't suppose to judge."

"Who says a therapist isn't supposed to
judge?"

"It's common knowledge?"

"Whose common knowledge?"

Dumbfounded and confused, the patient
backed down. When he returned for his individual
session that week he was full of rage. He said he
had discussed the group session with friends and
they had agreed that it was not right for a therapist
to judge and insult a patient. "It just wasn't right!"

"Well," the analyst said. "I discussed it with

myself and I don't think it's right for you to talk about women the way you do." She had prepared herself for his protest.

"But I have a right to say whatever I want to say in therapy without being verbally abused."

"And I have the right to say whatever I want to say," the analyst countered, "without being verbally abused by you."

"I'm not verbally abusing you."

"You verbally abuse me and all women just about every time you open your mouth."

"There you go, judging me again."

"Just like you judge women."

"This is ridiculous."

"Yes it is."

"If you're not going to listen to me, I'm leaving."

"I don't take kindly to threats."

The patient left before the hour was over, slamming the door behind him. He never returned.

In this case once again the analyst became involved in a sadomasochistic struggle with the patient and was able to rationalize it under the rubric of modern analysis. On an unconscious level, she wanted to injure the patient and to get rid of him. His badmouthing of the women he dated aroused an unresolved anger and envy of men and of male privilege. In addition to the therapist's characterological counterresistance, she was also acting out cultural counterresistance linked with both modern analytic and feminist ideologies.

Obviously, I have presented rather dramatic instances of counterresistance in this chapter. Not all classical psychoanalysts, self psychologists, or modern analysts are this errant and in fact, most tend to err in much less dramatic ways. I use these examples to make my point more clearly.

A general rule of practically all schools of therapy is that the therapist should not do anything to harm a patient. If the therapist is passive, the passivity should not have malice; if the therapist is empathic, the empathy should not be of the appeasing, hence provoking, variety; if the therapist is confrontational, the confrontation should be firm, but without animosity. Just as the therapist uses feelings the patient has induced to determine what is going on in the patient's head, so, too, the patient can use the feelings induced by the therapist to determine what is in the therapist's head. If the patient feels harmed by the therapist, then often the therapist wants to harm the patient.

When looking at counterresistance, one can view it from the therapist's point of view, from the patient's point of view, from the view of a third party, or from the view of somebody from Mars. The famous Japanese movie, *Rashomon*, portrayed this phenomenon, retelling the story of a murder and rape from four different perspectives without ever being able to uncover an objective truth. It is just as difficult at times to distinguish objective from subjective counterresistance.

The literature on counterresistance has not been of much help in this regard. Nearly all of it has been scholarly and abstract. Indeed, it may be argued that highly abstract psychoanalytic writings about countertransference and counterresistance that focus on minutiae about internalized

object relations, ego defenses, restitutive structures, and projective identifications are in and of
themselves part of the problem. They pretend to
study counterresistance but in reality defend it by
making it an abstraction rather than something
actual and specific. This is akin to a patient who
talks in abstract terms about a problem with his
sex life, and never gets to the point.

I have tried to reverse this trend by offering
concrete case histories whose meaning and emotional impact are unobstructed by psychoanalytic
terminology.

**8**

---

# Counterresistance
# in Groups

Groups present more complex problems with regard to both resistance and counterresistance. In a group the therapist has to deal not only with the resistance of each of his patients, but also with the group resistance as a whole. The therapist will thus be hit by many resistances at once and, unless he or she stays on top of the intense countertransference feelings the group induces, as well as the impulses to counterresist, a group can easily go astray.

Not only do the group members utilize differing defenses—representing various transference, characterological, or cultural resistances both toward each other and toward the therapist—but they also witness the ways each member resists and how the therapist reacts to each resistance. They notice if the therapist favors one member or one sex. They notice if the therapist is hostile to one or more members or if he overprotects a member. They notice what kind of behavior upsets the therapist and how the therapist reacts to it. In other words, the group situation provides many new ways for both patients and therapists to resist the therapy process.

Just as in individual therapy it is the therapist's counterresistance that must be analyzed first and is most crucial to the success or failure of the therapy, so too in group therapy success rests on the therapist's capacity to analyze his counterresistance to the individual members and to the group as a whole. And, because of the complexity of the operation, the therapist must be even more aware at all times of the feelings the group is arousing and of his or her effect on the group.

"All progress in group treatment parallels the analyst's discovery of his own inner life as prompted by his or her patients," Ormont writes (1992, p. 81). Viewing group therapy as a learning experience for both the therapist and members, he adds, "By relying on what goes on in group for our own self-understanding, we are best able to help the members" (p. 82).

In addition to the three types of counterresistance that occur in individual therapy, there is another kind of resistance and counterresistance that occurs in groups: It might be called, simply, group transference resistance and group countertransference resistance. Insofar as groups are like families, participants tend to play the role in groups that they played in their families; that is, the group arouses a particular kind of resistance from each participant. One member, for example, may play the mother, protecting other members from the bad father (the leader), duplicating a role she played in her family. Another plays the clown. Another plays the defiant child. Another plays the problem-solver, another the peacemaker, another the prince or princess.

In addition, the group arouses a particular kind of counterresistance from the therapist, which depends on the previous family role of the therapist. Therapists who were the eldest in their families and grew up assuming a leadership role may easily assume that role in a group. The scapegoat of the family may tend to feel unworthy of confronting an aggressive member and be persecuted by him. The therapist idealized or doted on by his parents may want the group to idealize or dote on him. The enabler of a parent's alcoholism may unwittingly fall into that role.

Because of the intense feelings that a group arouses, a therapist may be quickly drawn into a form of counterresistance without knowing it. At any one time there are a multitude of currents and crosscurrents in the group that the therapist must react to and deal with. He or she must constantly make split decisions that may affect the outcome of the group. At each step of the way something may go wrong, and if one thing does go wrong—if one member develops a group-destructive resistance, for example—the rest of the group may quickly become infected.

The potential for emotional contagion is much stronger in groups than in individual therapy. A group may catch "the laughs" and it can also catch "the cries" or "the silence" or "the jitters" or "let's blame the therapist." The therapist must be able to tap in and nip potential negative contagion in the bud. Figure 8–1 provides a chart of the myriad resistances and counterresistances that arise in a typical group.

## THE DOUBLE-BINDING GROUP THERAPIST

In groups, more than in individual therapy, the therapist must be a leader; as a leader, he must take an active role in such matters as mediating disputes among members, dealing with the various group-destructive resistances, and generally regulating the group. Sometimes this involves the use of manipulation (or, an objective form of counterresistance). One of the most common kinds of manipulation used by therapists is the double bind.

Zen masters use the double bind objectively. They will hold a stick over a pupil's head and say menacingly, "If you say this stick is real, I will strike you with it. If you say it is not real, I will strike you with it. If you don't say anything, I will strike you with it." What the Zen master wants is to stimulate the pupil toward finding a way out of the double bind. If the student grabs the stick from the master, the master bows and smiles.

Bateson and colleagues (1981) noted the constructive uses of the double bind in Zen and therapy, but also pointed out its destructive use in dysfunctional families. In such families, parents

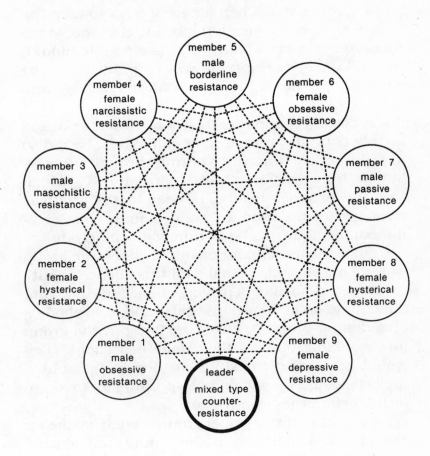

Note: In a group of nine members and one leader, there would be ninety resistances and counterresistances going at the same time, of different varieties, as shown.

**Figure 8.1.** The Complexity of Resistance in Groups

put children into double binds from which they cannot find an escape which, of course, leads to psychopathology. When a parent says to a crying little boy, "Stop your crying or I'll give you something to really cry about," this is a double bind. If the child keeps crying, he will be punished. If he stops crying, he will have to stuff his feelings and not be able to complete his mourning.

A certain group therapist was prone to putting members of his group into double binds. He did so in order to facilitate the working through process, but at times his narcissistic grandiosity, which took the form of a need to be seen by the group as an omniscient shaman, undermined (or overmined) his ability to be in tune with the group.

On one occasion, for example, when the group was silent, he said, "What's all this silence about? I feel a lot of hostile, depriving silence in the room. John just spilled out his guts and everybody's abandoning him." In effect, he had put the group into a double bind; if they remained silent, they would be labeled "hostile and depriving," but if they spoke up, they would be speaking up involuntarily, before they wanted to.

Several group members immediately spoke up and gave feedback to John. One young man, blurted out, "I think there's something strange going on in the group. Everybody was laughing before the silence, the way people do after funerals."

"Are you being critical of the group?" the therapist asked.

"No," the man said. "I'm not being critical of the group. I was just making an observation."

"Is it helpful to make such an observation?" the therapist persisted.

"I don't know," the man said, getting flustered. "You said for people to speak up, so I just said the first thing that came into my head."

The therapist turned to another person, and the man sat back and began to feel angry with him. A sensitive young man with strong masochistic features, and he experienced the therapist as attacking him unfairly, and he was right. The therapist had used a double bind to end the silence, then attacked the patient with an interpretation, which made the therapist look clever and the patient feel stupid. This played right into the patient's masochistic process. For several sessions after that, the patient came to the group late and sulked in silence. After he finally broke out of his slump and the therapist acknowledged that he had inadvertently attacked him, there still remained a barrier in the therapeutic alliance.

The therapist had not helped the patients work through the resistance that had caused the silence; instead he had manipulated them out of the silence. Therapeutic manipulation is most often a form of counterresistance, unless it is done by a skilled and aware therapist who knows what he is doing and why. Through subjective therapeutic manipulation, the therapist acts out a narcissistic need to prove his prowess and an obsessive-compulsive impatience with letting things evolve naturally.

## THE GROUP LEADER AS CLOWN

Some group leaders, because they have an audience, become entertainers. Indeed, therapists who are most drawn to leading groups are often narcissistic, with exhibitionistic features. The group plays into their idealized image of themselves and, like entertainers, they feed off their audience's adulation. Soon quips are rolling off their tongues, expressions are flashing from their brows, and they become the life of the group. The group, in such cases, joins the therapist's counterresistance, glad to turn the work of the group into a humorous outing rather than into the more serious therapy. However, this kind of collusion is at the expense of the group, and because it is so entertaining, its destructiveness is not readily discernible.

Back in the 1970s, I became acquainted with a Gestalt therapist who quoted funny lines from Shakespeare, Blake, and Eliot, wiggling his eyebrows as he did so, à la Groucho Marx. He had a favorite in the group who served as his straight man, and every so often during a session he would turn to the straight man and say, "You know what Shakespeare said about sex, don't you James?"

James would glibly answer, "No, but I'm sure you'll tell me."

"How swell of you to ask," the therapist would reply, smirking.

"Think everything of it, kind sir," James would grin.

"Don't mention it, my good man," the therapist would answer, wiggling his brows once more for good measure.

They would go on like that, two buddies entertaining, while at the same time excluding, the "troops." These asides were brief and enjoyable, but they interrupted the flow of the group and diverted it away from areas to which the therapist had a counterresistance. In addition, this exclusive buddy relationship factionalized the group and created, in effect, two classes, with the therapist and his sidekick at the top and the rest at the bottom. This created resentments and jealousies that eventually led to flare-ups, the therapist invariably analyzed the transference of those who were angry with the sidekick, while letting James go unanalyzed.

This clown-therapist also ridiculed certain members to the group. This was done in fun and in such subtle ways that nobody thought about it. One woman in the group, Daphne, would ask foolish questions. The therapist would play off these questions the way Groucho Marx did in the movies and on television. The woman would ask a question and he would turn to the group, rolling back his eyes, and say, "Let me see, how can I answer that question. I can't for the life of me come up with an answer. . . . James, help me out here. Daphne wants to know whether therapists are human. Can you answer that question for her?"

"You know what T. S. Eliot says about that, don't you?" James would reply, satirical.

"I wasn't aware that T. S. Eliot said anything about therapists."

"You're quite mistaken."

"What, sir, did he say, pray tell?"

This repartee would continue for a few minutes and the group would be charmed into laughter, including Daphne, even though the laugh was on her. In such instances her masochism would induce the therapist's sadism, and vice versa.

Having grown used to being the goat of her family's jokes, she now played that role in the group. Having grown used to being the sadistic clown-prince of his family, the therapist now played that role as group leader. He and Daphne enacted their roles and stayed stuck in a resistance and counter-resistance duet that precluded genuine relating, working through, and maturation.

Partly because of the therapist's example and partly because she truly could be irritating to the group through her masochistic provocations, other group members dismissed Daphne as a "nut," which meant that her feelings were not taken seriously. When they ridiculed her, however, the therapist came to her defense. He gave a mixed signal; on the one hand he would ridicule Daphne himself, and on the other hand he would appear to defend her. One signal nullified the other, and the group paid no attention.

Eventually Daphne began to grow more and more frustrated and to lash out at the group for not treating her with respect. When she did, the leader would look at her and say, "How can we treat you with respect when you constantly act the fool?" Or he would give her an interpretion about her re-peating pattern and how she had learned as a child to provoke disrespect from others. He did not take responsibility for his part in encouraging her to act the fool, nor did the rest of the group.

Just as parents in a family may displace re-sentment and anger toward each other onto their children, so too members of a group often displace their antagonism onto a scapegoat; Daphne served as group scapegoat. If one of the members was angry at James, he might take it out on Daphne, knowing that the leader would protect James but not Daphne. In the end, Daphne angrily left the group without any real insight into what had happened to her or why. When she left the leader and other members of the group were sorry to lose her only because there would no longer be anybody around on whom to project and displace their negativity, and they were all sure that her inability to function in the group was due entirely to her own neurosis.

This was a case of a therapist's characterological counterresistance and a group's resistance joining up and becoming intensified by the emotional contagion of the group. The primary source of this resistance was the therapist's own narcissism and underlying rage. His clowning was a defense he had learned in his own family, where the direct expression of aggression was not permitted, but indirect expressions such as clowning were applauded. In his own family, ridicule was an accepted form of aggression; his parents ridiculed each other and his older brother, who in turned ridiculed him. He in turn ridiculed his younger sister, who had moved far away from the rest of the family after she left home, just as Daphne now moved away from the group.

The therapist had had years of training therapy. He knew all about his role in his family and how his clowning served a defensive function. Nevertheless, the group situation revived this defensive impulse, which sprang to the surface almost reflexively. No matter how much therapy or supervision one has, one's basic character cannot be completely changed. When situations occur that replicate the situations that originally created the defense, the defense will tend to reemerge, though perhaps with less conviction.

## THE ABSENT GROUP AND THE GREEDY THERAPIST

Soon after a group had been formed, its members began coming late and missing sessions. The members of the group, primarily high-powered business people, seemed to see the group as secondary to their business pursuits. Of the seven people in the group, generally only four or five showed up for the weekly session. On one occasion, only two members showed up, and the therapist became alarmed.

"What's going on?" he asked the group the following week. "There seems to be a lot of resistance in the group. A lot of lateness and a lot of absences."

For a while everybody was silent. Then, one by one people began to speak up.

"It's not resistance," a corporate lawyer said. "I've simply had a heavy caseload this month, and I've been working overtime every night and on weekends. It just can't be avoided. Sorry."

"I've had one emergency after another at my stores," a retailer said. "Nobody seems to know what to do about it, so I have to go down and take care of it. That's really all it is."

"Last session my baby-sitter got sick and I

couldn't find another one," a woman manager said. "I just couldn't get away."

The other members had similar excuses.

"But why couldn't you call in? You know you always have the option to call in and participate in the group over the speaker phones."

"I feel strange doing that," the woman said.

"I just couldn't get to a phone," the lawyer said.

"But what about the lateness," the therapist persisted.

"Couldn't find a parking space," the lawyer said.

"Exactly," the manager said. "It's a tough neighborhood for parking. It really is."

The therapist was furious when he reported to his supervision group. "I don't know what to do about this group. I feel like strangling them all. I feel like just ending the group and telling them all to go to hell." Upon analyzing the situation, it turned out that the therapist was charging a very high fee for the group, higher than he had ever charged before. Hence, he felt guilty about the fee and was trying too hard to make the group a success and earn the money he was charging. Then, as the group began to act out its absentee resistance, he grew anxious about losing the group and the considerable monthly income it provided for him.

"The group has a resistance and you have a counterresistance," the supervisor said. "The group's pulling one way and you're pulling the other. They're saying, 'We're not particularly interested in this group, not particularly interested in you,' and you're saying, 'Why aren't you interested in the group? Why aren't you interested in me? I want you to be interested in being here.' There's a resistance–counterresistance struggle."

How was the therapist drawn into this struggle? First of all, he had overextended himself by charging more than he felt comfortable charging. His greed had overruled his reason (his superego via its ideal image had overruled his ego). From a psychodynamic point of view, his characterological need to be a financial success stemmed from an oedipal desire to defeat his father and brothers. The phallic-narcissistic features of his personality had taken command of his psyche. The group members had become transference objects to him, and on this level he wanted to conquer them by charging them a high price and forcing them to see how valuable and superior he was. However, he then felt guilty about defeating his rivals. The group members, unconsciously picking up his need to conquer them, his arrogance, his insecurity, and his guilt, responded by resisting and, in effect, telling him to "go to hell."

Fortunately, the supervision group was able to help the therapist see all this and to find a way out of the situation. The supervisor advised him to let go of his fury and join the group's resistance. He pointed out that it was almost time for the summer vacation and recommended breaking early. "Tell the group that there seems to be a problem with respect to members attending the group, but don't go into any analysis because they're not ready for that. Just say there seems to be a problem . . . perhaps the group should break up early. That would give people time to straighten out their business affairs and decide if they really have time for and want the group. When the group meets again in the fall members can discuss whether they want to continue or discontinue the group."

The therapist followed the supervisor's suggestion. When the group returned in the fall, the members were unanimous in wanting to continue the group, and absenteeism virtually ceased. By joining their resistance, the group therapist had overcome his own counterresistance. He gave the message that he did not need the money and that it was their group to build or destroy.

## THE THERAPIST WHO NEEDED TO BE ACCEPTED

Needing approval is a handicap for a therapist in individual therapy, but in a group it is a liability. One group therapist was continually starting groups only to see them fall apart after a few months. None of them lasted more than a year. Yet he persisted.

This therapist had suffered a great deal of shame in his family as he was growing up, and as a result he had a need to create new families in which he might be accepted, even admired, to counteract the shame and scorn of his childhood. However, his repeated attempts to form these families were destined to end in failure. It did not take long for members of the group to catch on that the therapist needed their acceptance. He continually gratified requests to come late, to miss sessions, to skip payments when they said they were in financial straits, and to avoid dealing with painful feelings. Although he encouraged the members to express negative feelings, when they did so he would rush in with a defensive interpretation that prevented the full blossoming of the negative transference. He thereby gave a nonverbal message that he would be hurt if they expressed negative feelings.

For a few months he would get the acceptance and love he asked for. But soon the members were missing more sessions, skipping more payments, and generally becoming more and more resistant. Much of their resistance, if not most, was in response to the therapist's characterological counterresistance. Because of his need to always come off as a "nice guy," he was reluctant to maintain control of the group, enforce the fee policy, and confront members about their resistance.

In this case, the group therapist's continued failed attempts to form groups represented his repetition compulsion, his attempt to undo what was done in childhood. There was the unconscious hope, when he formed each new group, that this time the members would realize what a good and valuable person he was. But no group could ever give him the acceptance that he had yet to give himself.

## GROUP SYSTEMS THEORY

These examples of counterresistance in groups are some of the most common and overt kinds. There are many more subtle forms. Overt or subtle, these examples underscore the fact that therapy groups are systems, just like families. In order for a family or group to work well, its system must be in smooth working order. Its rules must be viable and enforced, and these rules must be based upon sound values.

When a family becomes dysfunctional, family systems theory holds that there is a fault in the system, and not in any one member of the family. Generally there is one member in the family who is doing most of the acting out (resisting), but upon closer inspection it invariably turns out that the member who is doing the acting out is being affected by a complex system of dysfunctional communication in the family as a whole.

In groups, one or more of the members may appear to be the most troublesome and dysfunctional, but upon closer inspection it will be revealed that the system of communication in the group is at fault. The leader is responsible for maintaining the system, but all members contribute to it. A group therapist, therefore, must always keep an eye on the overall system as well as on the individuals in the system.

# 9

# Counterresistance and the Transference Neurosis

In classical psychoanalytic literature, the transference neurosis is considered to be an essential, if not *the* essential aspect of psychoanalytic cure. Freud (1914, p. 150) called it "a new edition of the old disease." It was his contention, and that of his followers, that transference could be divided into roughly two phases, the first being that of transient displacement of feelings from the original parents or other significant persons, the second being a more intense phase in which the compulsion repetition takes over completely and the so-called infantile neurosis (Oedipus complex) reoccurs, this time in relation to the therapist.

"We render the compulsion harmless, and indeed useful, by giving it the right to assert itself in a definite field," Freud notes. He goes on to assert that once the compulsion has emerged in all its facets, "we regularly succeed in giving all the symptoms of the illness a new transference meaning and in replacing his ordinary neurosis by a 'transference-neurosis' of which he can be cured by the therapeutic work" (p. 154). In other words, Freud believed that the transference neurosis represented the patient's neurosis coming to a boil in the transference, and it was while it was at its most heated and irrational that the most therapeutic progress could be made. At the same time, he also believed that the more an analyst frustrated a patient's desires by being abstinent, the more this transference neurosis could be hastened.

Today, one does not read very much about transference neuroses. In fact, Freud himself did not write about them after 1920. Freud and other psychoanalytic writers began to realize that not all, and not even most, patients would develop a transference neurosis, while some developed such an intense transference resistance (the term transference psychosis was introduced by Margaret Little to describe this more disturbed version) that it was beyond the reach of analysis. This eventually led to Eissler's (1953) famous paper on parameters, in which he introduced a new distinction between analyzable and nonanalyzable patients, along with variations of the abstinence rule.

Greenson (1978) pointed out how the therapist's working alliance affects the transference neurosis. In order for the transference neurosis to be resolved, the therapist and patient must have a strong working alliance. "We induce the patient to regress and to develop a transference neurosis by providing a situation that consists of a mixture of deprivation, a sleeplike condition, and constancy. . . . For a good therapeutic result, however, one must also achieve a good working relationship'' (p. 221). Greenson was on the right track.

My own experience had caused me to question whether or not a transference neurosis is truly the crucial condition of therapeutic change, and to wonder whether, in fact, it is sometimes, perhaps even often, a virulent form of resistance that arises in response to a certain kind of psychoanalytic experience. In fact, I have come to believe that the transference neurosis is not the crucial condition of change, but only one permutation in the lengthy working-through process. There may be several periods during the course of a therapy when particular patients become overinvolved with the therapist that is, develop a transference neurosis. During these times, they love and hate the therapist with a new intensity and, at the same time, are vulnerable to the therapist's interpretations. However, even though these are intense periods and even though much lasting communication can occur during and after them, they are not in and of themselves the keys to successful treatment. The key is, as I said, the laborious day-to-day, week-to-week working-through process. Some patients, and some analysts, particularly in the early days of psychoanalysis, believed that after one such transference neurosis episode the patient was cured. This turned out not to be so.

Moreover, transference neuroses are in actuality rare nowadays and seem to occur only in certain situations: when the patient is in therapy at least three times a week, when he is undergoing a kind of treatment that involves a high degree of frustration and interpretation and when he has a higher-level neurotic or narcissistic personality capable of forming a good working alliance. The second condition—the frustration of the patient—is the factor that is most important. It is my contention that in many cases the therapist's counterresistance frustrates certain patients into a transference neurosis unnecessarily, when the same results might have been achieved through a therapist's slowly and quietly inspiring the patient's love and trust. Indeed, it has even occurred to me that the heralding of the transference neurosis in the early days of analysis was a way of denying and rationalizing psychoanalytic passive aggression.

Kohut's first analysis with Mr. Z. provides one example this. When the working alliance was not good, when Kohut was using what he described as classical analytic techniques without empathy, Mr. Z. developed more of a transference neurosis, was constantly in a rage at Kohut, constantly complaining, and constantly making unrealistic demands on him. Kohut thought that by resolving this transference neurosis he had cured Mr. Z., but he was wrong. In his second analysis the therapist and patient developed more of a loving, trusting bond, and there was, it appeared, much less of a transference neurosis, if any at all. Hence, the transference neurosis appears to have been entirely brought about by the therapist's counterresistance.

## FREUD AND THE RAT MAN

Freud's treatment of the Rat Man, whose first name was Ernst, provides an another example of this idea. Ernst entered treatment with Freud at the age of 30, suffering from a severe obsessive-compulsive neurosis. He was born in 1878, the son of a mother who came from a wealthy industrial family and a father who was a low- ranking military officer. He had three older sisters, a younger brother, and two younger sisters. His father died when Ernst was 21 years old, and it was at that time that his obsessive symptoms began to appear. However, during his 20s he managed to get a law degree, not without difficulty and delay, and to become enamored of an older woman who did not return his affections. Later, during a military exercise in which he took part as a reserve officer, an incident occurred that stoked his obsessive neurosis to an even greater extent and sent him to Freud's office.

From the beginning, Ernst gave Freud unmistakable clues as to the nature and source of his obsessive neurosis and of his transference resistance. In the first session, Ernst spoke at length about his relations with two older men who had become mentors to him. One of these men had turned on him and now treated him as if he were an idiot. Freud observed that Ernst's words "laid stress upon the influence exercised over him by men, that is to say, upon the part played in his life by homosexual object-choice . . ." (1909, p. 159). However, he apparently did not understand the implications with regard to the resistance and counterresistance. Ernst was telling Freud that he wanted him to be like the friend he trusted, not like the man who had turned on him. He wanted Freud to be a kindly, knowing, preoedipal father, not a rivalrous oedipal father who would turn on him.

Later in that first session Ernst recalled child-

hood voyeuristic fantasies and thoughts and recounted his fears that his parents could read his
mind. Whenever as a child he had such sexual
fantasies, he would have the obsessive thought
that if his father guessed what he was fantasizing
about, his father would die. This again was a
statement to Freud about the nature of his transference; he did not want Freud to be intrusive like
his father and probe into his thoughts, for such
intrusiveness was to him a life or death matter.
Freud might guess that Ernst wanted to kill him.

In the second session, Freud disregarded these
clues and proceeded to become quite intrusive.
Ernst began to relate the famous incident about the
rats. That summer, he told Freud with difficulty,
he had been required, as an officer of the reserve, to
take part in maneuvers. He wanted very much to
prove himself to the regular officers, "to show the
regular officers that people like me had not only
learned a good deal but could stand a good deal
too" (p. 165). He was so eager to prove himself that
when he lost his lorgnette during a rest stop he did
not even stop to look for it; instead he wired his
optician to send another by postal express. During
the rest he sat next to a captain toward whom he
felt a dread, and who was "fond of cruelty," a man
with whom Ernst had had a prior argument about
corporal punishment. Now, as he sat with this
dreaded captain, the latter began telling him about
a specially horrible punishment he had read about,
used in the East.

As he got to this part of the story, Ernst leaped
up from the couch and began to pace around the
office in a stage of agitation. "Please, spare me a

recital of the details. Please," he told Freud (p. 166).

Freud assured Ernst that unlike Captain M. he had absolutely no taste for cruelty and had no intention of tormenting him unnecessarily. This was one of his first mistakes, the first "symptom" of Freud's own developing counterresistance. Why did Freud need to defend himself and draw a distinction between himself and the captain? Such defensiveness could only succeed in planting more deeply in an obsessive person's mind the suspicion that Freud *was* like the captain (and like Ernst's instrusive father).

Ernst tried to continue to recall the captain's horrible story, which had to do with a form of torture in which rats were put against the naked buttocks of the victims. "They bored their way in," Ernst said, and then could go no further. At this point Freud finished the sentence for him: " . . . into his anus." In making this intervention Freud was not only being lulled into the role of the cruel torturer, but also identifying himself with the father who could read his son's mind. He had, in essence, penetrated Ernst with his psychoanalytic phallus. Indeed, Ernst went into such a daze that for the remainder of the session he began calling Freud "Captain."

Toward the end of the first week, Freud continued to "penetrate" Ernst with his psychoanalytic phallus. He began to insist repeatedly that Ernst had a death wish against his father. Ernst did not want to hear this at all, was not at all ready to hear it, but Freud persisted. "According to psychoanalytic theory," he told Ernst, "every wish corre-

sponds to a former wish which was not repressed"
(p. 180). Ernst said he loved his father very much.
Freud continued to probe and interrogate, and at
one point he announced, "You have just produced
the answer we were looking for" (p. 181). Ernst had
just uncovered "the third great characteristic of
the unconscious," the source from which his hostility to his father derived its indestructibility.
Ernst felt, Freud declared, that his father was
interfering with his sexual desires, and so he
wanted to get rid of him.

For days and weeks Freud harped on this
point. The father transference blossomed and the
resistance heated up, until in the third and fourth
months Ernst developed a transference neurosis.
"Things soon reached a point," Freud wrote, "at
which, in his waking phantasies, and his associations, he began heaping the grossest and filthiest
abuse upon me and my family, though in his
deliberate actions he never treated me with anything but the greatest respect" (p. 206). In the
middle of this transference neurosis, he brought in
a dream in which Freud's mother had died and he
was anxious to offer Freud his condolences, but he
was afraid that in doing so he might break into an
impertinent laugh. Freud interpreted that the
mother in the dream was really Ernst's mother,
and Ernst angrily asked if Freud was taking revenge on him with such interpretations. On another occasion, he saw a girl on Freud's stairway
and decided she was Freud's daughter; he imagined Freud wanted to match him up with her, and
draw him away from his lady friend, just as his
father had tried to do. "The only reason you're so

kind and patient with me," he told Freud, "is you want me for a son-in-law" (p. 198). He dreamed that he saw Freud's daughter in front of him and that she had two patches of dung for eyes. Freud interpreted that Ernst wished to marry his daughter not for her beautiful eyes, but for her money (excrement = money). Such interpretations ignored Ernst's transference wishes and oedipal impulses; therefore they could not resolve them and may have exacerbated the transference neurosis.

In the notes that were published posthumously (pp. 253–318), Freud described interventions that went beyond the scope of what is now called classical psychoanalysis, and which may have further exacerbated Ernst's transference neurosis. For example, he asked Ernest to bring in a photograph of his lady friend, and Ernst responded by threatening to quit the treatment, apparently viewing Freud's request as another attempt to interfere with his sexual life. On another occasion he fed Ernst herring, which took up a good portion of a session. Four sessions later Ernst complained that Freud had made a profit out of the meal, since Ernst had lost time because of it. Still later Freud lent Ernst a book, Emile Zola's *Joie de Vivre*, because the hero's problems resembled Ernst's. Again, Ernst voiced suspicion of Freud's motives. Freud seemed to vacillate from frustrating Ernst with his interpretations to gratifying him with food and books, which was perhaps an expression of his own ambivalent counterresistance.

Throughout it all, Ernst grew angrier and angrier and then felt guilty about his acting out.

"How can a gentleman like you, sir," he asked, "let yourself be abused in this way by a low, good-for-nothing wretch like me? You ought to turn me out: that's all I deserve" (p. 206). It was clear that Ernst had an unconscious need to be kicked out of therapy, to resist the storms of feelings that were arising in him and undoubtedly in Freud as well. The trouble was, Freud never acknowledged his own feelings.

Freud's failure to respond to Ernst in a more authentic way perhaps caused Ernst's verbal assaults to grow more intense. Now Ernst began to bury his head in his hands or to jump up from the couch and roam about the room. When Freud asked why he did that, he answered, "I'm afraid you'll give me a beating" (p. 206). At last Ernst got in touch with his deepest layers of fear of Freud, and of his father, who had given him savage beatings as a child. But it had taken a long time and the patient had been pushed to the limit. Was it all necessary?

Kanzer (1980, p. 238) has pointed out a similarity between Ernst's traumatic experience as a child and Freud's. When Ernst was beaten by his father during the oedipal stage, he responded by heaping verbal abuse on the father, and the father had then snorted, "The child will either be a great man or a great criminal." When Freud was 8 years old he urinated on his parents' bedroom floor, and his father exclaimed, "This boy will come to nothing." Freud later said that this incident haunted him for the rest of his life, and lay behind his accomplishments, as though he were saying to his father, "You see, I have amounted to something after all." In both instances, self-assertion to the father at the height of the oedipal period was "the occasion for substitutive castration and change in personality" (p. 238).

I would add that the similarity of Freud's case and that of Ernst aroused Freud's counterresistance. Because Freud had not completely come to grips with his oedipal anger and guilt toward his father, though he made a brave attempt to do so in his self-analysis, he could not tolerate Ernst's feelings. He had a need to complete sentences for him, to give interpretations, to appease him, to gratify him, and to indoctrinate him intellectually. When Ernst began his story about the cruel rat torture, it may have rekindled similar fantasies that Freud had had. When Ernst verbalized a death wish against Freud's mother, Freud may have felt protective of his mother and responded with an interpretation that contained a death wish against the patient's mother.

Freud kept interfering in Ernst's love life despite Ernst's warnings that he should not interfere as his father had done. What compelled Freud to do so? To behave toward a patient in a way that a therapist knows will upset the patient is sadistic in a passive-aggressive way. Freud appeared to be helpful by asking to see a photograph of the lady friend, and by giving him a book to read, but the patient experienced him as intrusive and interfering. To pretend to be nice and helpful when in fact one is being aggressive puts a patient in a double bind and induces feelings of confusion, helplessness, and rage. If somebody appears to be helpful, how can you express rage to him? Yet, if you do not, you must block the feelings and doubt your own perspective. Hence, Freud's countersistance contributed to Ernst's confusion, guilt, and rage, and pushed him to the brink. When Ernst cried out, "How can a gentleman like you, sir, let yourself be abused in this way by a low, good-for-nothing wretch like me?" Perhaps he was really asking, "Are you really being nice to me, or is something else going on here? Talk to me!"

The treatment lasted a little over eleven months. According to Freud, Ernst's obsessional neurosis was cured once the rat obsession was solved. He adds, however, that after Ernst's funds had dwindled they agreed to termination. We have no way of knowing whether the "cure" was permanent, since Ernst was killed in World War I.

## THE BICYCLE MAN

The case of the Rat Man brings to mind one of my own cases that got out of hand because I unwittingly provoked a transference neurosis.

The Bicycle Man came to me a few years ago complaining that he had been drifting through life without ever examining it. When I mentioned the notion of bringing in dreams, he replied, "I only sleep three or four hours a night, and I've never remembered a single dream. As far as I can tell, I don't dream at all."

"Everybody dreams," I said. "You just don't remember your dreams."

"So you think there's hope?"

"Absolutely."

A handsome man in his early thirties with a body that was tanned and muscled, he sat alertly before me, speaking with strained confidence. "I've spend my adulthood working day and night, making large sums of money, devoting myself almost totally to my work while neglecting my social life. I'm your typical workaholic. I've dated men and women, but I never really feel anything emotionally for the people I date. After a while, they become too demanding and I have to back off. All this has become boring to me of late. During the past year I've started to wonder where my life is heading, so I sold my businesses and am taking a year off to study acting and find myself. I don't know if I'll be able to bring in any dreams, though. Are you sure everybody dreams?"

What his dreams and his free associations revealed was a lonely young man who could not relate to anybody because he was still quite attached, in a destructive way, to his parents, who had stunted his development and trained him to become a narcissistic extension of themselves. He was their golden boy who would achieve great things in life that would reflect on them. Before entering therapy, he had attempted to live out their fantasy, working 14-hour days and amassing a small fortune, remaining distant and superior to all who tried to relate to him on a personal level.

His parents had both spoiled and overprotected him, while urging him relentlessly toward achievements in school, which centered on good grades, and later on work. As a child he was discouraged from forming strong attachments outside the family, such as with neighborhood children, who might contaminate him, and later with adolescent girls, who might sexually entrap him. From what he told me about his aunts, uncles, and grandparents, this type of value system had gone on for generations without being questioned.

In the beginning his transference toward me was that of the obedient son. He performed therapy the way he might have organized a business venture: he threw himself into it in a very organized fashion, attending three times a week, and expected to get immediate results. He appeared to make good strides, getting in touch with a great deal of anger about his parents, learning to dream, and withdrawing from a destructive relationship. I helped him to assert and individuate himself from his parents and encouraged him to set up a therapy session with his immediate family that proved fruitful. He spoke frequently of how much therapy had helped him, and positively about my interventions. Then things began going awry.

More and more he began to say he did not think he was making any more progress. More and more he began to compare me to his father. More and more he began acting out anger toward me in subtle ways.

"I think therapy is making me worse instead of better," he said one day.

"How's that?"

"It's just making me worse. I don't know why. Maybe because you just sit back there behind the couch and ask me questions like 'how's that?'"

"What should I be doing?"

"I don't know what you should be doing! You're the therapist, you should know what to do!"

We had many renditions of this same inter-change and he became more and more frustrated. Truthfully, I really did not know what to do. So he began to challenge me more and more. He would come in late and if I asked him what was going on he would answer in a belligerent way that he didn't think it was working so what did it matter. He began speaking of going to see another therapist. When I said that was certainly his option, he spat back that he knew that was his option and he did not need me to tell him that. He mentioned my similarity to his father and I attempted to interpret his negative father transference and he angrily refuted it. His hostility became more and more blatant—he came late, missed sessions, attacked my character, doubted that I had ever really helped anybody, and accused me of trying to cultivate dependency and exploit him emotionally and mon-etarily. It became a full-blown transference neuro-sis.

One day, he rolled his bicycle into my office. He had never asked my permission to bring a bicycle into my office, but there he was, a belligerent, I-dare-you-to-say-something grimace on his face. I found myself feeling enraged by this behavior and paralyzed by this rage. So I said nothing.

"I've decided to see another therapist. She uses massage and body work and is warm, not cold and rejecting like you," he said.

"You see me as cold and rejecting?," I mut-tered.

"That's what I just said."

"How am I cold and rejecting?"

"There you go with your questions again!"

I lapsed into silence, again paralyzed with feelings of rage and confusion.

"So do you think I should go to this therapist?"

"If you think that's what will help, then of course that's what you should do."

"Fuck you. You're just like my father. Always pretending to be warm and giving. You don't really want me to go to this other therapist. You're just saying that. I wish you'd either be genuinely happy for me or tell me you hate me for going to this therapist, instead of this phony shit."

The bicycle man soon after called to say he was stopping therapy and that he was going to see the massage therapist. I was unable to save the relationship.

In retrospect I realized that I had not been able to give him the responses that he needed due to my own countertransference. From the moment he entered my office, he frightened me. He reminded me of one of my older siblings, and I began to relate to him as I did this older sibling. I attempted to appease him and contain him. In the beginning this worked all right because he was seeking somebody with whom to ally himself against his parents, who were opposed to his coming to New York to be an actor. As long as he needed me as an ally, things went well. But after his therapy session with his family, he began to feel guilty about confronting them, and he then began displacing all his anger at them on me. Now I became a negative transference object and my attempts to appease and contain him through encouraging questions and defensive interpretations about his negative transference got nowhere. What he needed from me then, I think, was a genuine emotional inter-change. His complaints about my being cold and rejecting and phony were clues that he wanted a real, human communication with me, not "endless questions" and interpretations.

Had I said to him, for example, "You know, I'm finding myself feeling enraged by you, and I don't know why," this might have opened the door to the exploration of my counterresistance and allowed us to begin to resolve the budding impasse before it became a full-blown transference neurosis. I do not think that one has to wait until a transference neurosis is in full sway before one can successfully intervene. In fact, this is the most hazardous way to do therapy. It is much more effective, when the patient begins to express the negative transference feelings, to immediately pay attention to the pa-tient's underlying complaints ("You're cold and rejecting") and to address those complaints in the way that the patient wants them to be addressed (in this case through a real, emotional communica-tion).

I was unable to do so because the patient had immediately aroused a sibling countertransfer-ence, and his growing negativity toward me made me fear him, as I had once feared my sibling, and try all the more to appease and contain him. It had never worked with my sibling and it did not work with him. When a patient smells fear in a therapist, he will invariably act out all the more.

And so it had become a vicious cycle of attacks and counterattacks (in the guise of therapeutic interventions). At the height of all this I was not thinking very much about my own counterresistance, but of his resistance and how I could analyze it, how I could interpret it, and how I could get it resolved so that I could get him off my back.

## FALLING IN LOVE AND THE TRANSFERENCE NEUROSIS

It seems to me that in this case and in others, the therapist's counterresistance is the crucial factor in stimulating a transference neurosis. From the standpoint of passive–aggressive characterology, the therapist feels a sense of power and control by being able to provoke a patient into such a tizzy, all the while staying cool himself. We see this phenomenon often in married couples, when the man is an obsessive-compulsive of the passive–aggressive type, and the woman is a hysteric. The husband appears to give the wife everything, continually appeasing her, and yet she is continually having hysterical fits and complaining that the husband is depriving her. He generally *is* depriving her—of an authentic relationship.

Such was the case with Freud and Ernst, which points up what I said in the beginning chapter, and what Greenson has also stressed—the value of the real relationship as a counterpoint to the transference and countertransference relationship. My guess is that if Freud had himself been more integrated, and had therefore resolved his own father complex, he might have been able to be less intrusive and manipulative, and more authentic, toward Ernst. In that case, the transference neurosis would not have been a necessary part of the cure. Instead, it might be seen as an unnecessary detour brought by the therapist's counterresistance.

Another way of looking at the transference neurosis is to compare it with the tempestuous relationships of lovers as depicted in movies, plays, and novels. When people fall in love, they become intensely involved with one another. Each develops both an obsession with the other and a narcissistic overvaluation of the other. Sometimes this early infatuation fades into loving companionship. At other times it turns into a negative obsession with and a narcissistic devaluation of the other.

It is this kind of intense, ambivalent attachment that occurs in therapy and is called the transference neurosis. Undoubtedly there are times when one person can develop such an obsession toward another person, both in life and in the therapy office, without any help from the object of obsession. However, there are other times when the object of desire did in fact unconsciously encourage the obsession. A man sends a woman flowers and, even though she knows she is not interested in him, the flowers tickle her vanity. She is flattered. This encourages more flowers. Before long the man has developed an obsession and the woman says, "but I never wanted the flowers at all. Please get away from me!" This angers the man, who knows very well that she did want the flowers in the beginning, so he defiantly sends more flowers and flings himself at the woman as an act of spite. Eventually this leads to some kind of confrontation that again unconsciously, they may both want. While in some cases perhaps the transference neurosis develops by itself, I would guess that more often it is aided by the therapist's counterresistance.

**10**

---

# Counterresistance in the Afternoon: the Short, Unhappy Case of Mr. Snickler

"Is this—?" It was a young man's voice blurting out my name rather brashly over my phone.

"Yes it is."

"Are you the author of *Turning Points in Analytic Therapy?*"

"That's right."

"I just finished reading your book and I like it."

"Thanks."

"I was thinking that I'd like to try you out as a therapist."

"All right."

"Would it be possible to make an appointment today?

"No, I don't work on Friday."

"Do you work on Saturday?"

"No."

"Sunday?"

"No, I don't."

"I guess I'll try for Monday, then. What do you have on Monday?"

"I have 10 in the morning."

"Perfect." There seemed to be a smile of glee in his voice. "I'll see you then."

"Do you have my address?"

"Yes, it's in the telephone book. Don't worry, I'll find you. Bye-bye."

There are one-night stands and there are one-session stands. One-night stands, as everybody knows, are those one-night sexual encounters that used to happen more frequently in the pre-AIDS days—encounters that are noted for leaving one with feelings of dismay, disgust, disdain, and the fear of disease. One-session stands, as every therapist knows, are those one-session psychotherapy encounters that often leave therapists impaled with fear, loathing, murderous hate, unrequieted lust, and a few dozen other feelings. My encounter with "Mr. Snickler" (that, of course, is not his real name) was of the latter variety, although it was three sessions rather than one, and I still feel twinges of fear and loathing when I think of him.

He rang my doorbell at 10 A.M. sharp. Since he had read my book and had said he liked it, I expected somebody with a positive transference. But the young man who strode into my doorway had a glum expression on his face and glared at me as he passed by, sending immediate shockwaves through my body. He walked to the end of my office where my rocking chair sits and eyed the chair for a moment, as though making plans to confiscate it. I restrained myself from saying, "That's my chair, move the hell

away from it." He seemed to get the message, perhaps by mental telepathy, and pivoted abruptly, sitting down on the couch. Then he looked around at
the books on the far wall for a long time, as though
critically reviewing each one and finding them
lacking in depth and sophistication.

"So," I said, sitting proprietarily in my rocker.
"Are you a student?"

He scowled at me. "No. I'm not a student."

"I thought that since you had read my book
you were an analytic student."

"You thought wrong."

His tone of voice was contemptuous and cutting. I felt my body stiffen; I had not expected this.
However, my years of training in psychoanalysis
and of living in New York had conditioned me to be
prepared for anything. There was a silence. He
glanced around my room some more, checking out
my paintings, which he seemed to find equally
lacking in merit. I glanced around at the paintings
too, admiringly. He glared at me. I studied him.

"Why did you want to know if I'm a student?"
he asked.

"It seemed as good a place to start as any."

"I'm not a student. I'm not anything."

"You're not anything?"

"Right. I don't have an official position. I don't
go to school. I don't work. I live with my mother.
My mother supports me."

"How do you feel about that?"

"That's a typical shrink question. I love her
and I hate her. She's convenient. I use her and she
uses me." He looked at me. "I know, I know. You're
thinking that I have an Oedipus complex, that I

haven't separated from my mother, that I have a mother fixation.''

"Do you?"

"Who doesn't. Let's put it this way—you'll like this—my mother still comes into the bathroom to wash my back, and I'm 27 years old. I read your books because I've been searching for a therapist and because I like reading analytic books. I was in Barnes and Noble in the psychiatric section and I saw your books and they looked interesting. So I read a couple of them.''

"You only mentioned *Turning Points*."

"Yes, that's the one I had read when I called you. I liked it. I liked your knowledge of the field, and your dedication to it. Then I read one of your other books, *Sexual Animosity between Men and Women*, and I hated it.''

"You hated it?"

"That's right. I thought it was a bigoted, polemical diatribe against feminism.'' He looked at me with pointed disgust. "It was like something out of the Dark Ages, like some medieval tract against witches. When I finished it I thought about calling you back and canceling the appointment, but I decided to go ahead with it, since I liked your first book. Quite frankly, it was idiotic and sophomoric, and the argumentation in it was pure sophistry.'' He looked at me again. "I kept thinking about my mother. She's an avid feminist, and I hope she never picks up your book. If she does, she'll probably be really offended. It's such a nasty book.''

I felt my body stiffen again and saw words swimming through my mind, words of defense like, "Well, you're obviously such a narrow-minded and self-righteous and politically correct elitist nerd. . . ." I wanted to crush him intellectually, emotionally, and spiritually. Then I had a fantasy of meeting his mother. I envisoned a plump woman with round, metal-framed glasses and buggy brown eyes, clad in silver earrings that portrayed female biological symbols, coming at me with a 38-caliber pistol. I imagined myself wrenching the gun from her and wrestling her to the floor of my office, with her jumping back up and asking how I could write such sexist trash and sell it to her son. I snapped, "Why don't you let go of him?" She hissed into my ear that the trouble was that my mother did not train me well enough, and I replied, "You mean like you've trained your son?" She hammered my chest with her fists and I grabbed both arms and held them and she grinned defiantly and snorted, "What're you going to do now?"

I came back to the room and it began to dawn on me that I was hurt and angry and that Mr. Snickler was not exactly the admirer I had expected. I decided to join the resistance by yielding to it. "That really hurts," I said. "The things you're saying about my book. I worked very hard to write that book and I put all my heart into it, and it really hurts to hear somebody tear it down."

For a moment he glanced at me, oddly. He had not expected a therapist to admit he was hurt. But he quickly composed himself. "Well, you shouldn't have attacked women like that. If you're going to make such sniveling attacks on women, then you have to expect a counterattack."

"*Sniveling*? That really hurts." I was not acting. I was really hurt, but there was also a part of me that was still in control, objectively offering up my hurt as a chess player might offer a sacrificial pawn. "Why are you doing this?"

"It was an idiotic, vindictive, sniveling vendetta under the guise of being a scholarly work. Pure right-wing propaganda."

"Right wing?" I blurted. "Ouch!"

"Yes, right wing. I'm sorry, but that's how I feel."

He fell silent again and looked down. I mirrored him by falling silent and looking down as well. Out of the corner of my eyes I saw that the anger in his face and body had begun to recede and had been replaced by gloom. He sank down in the chair and his face took on a brooding aspect. Several minutes passed.

"What're you thinking?"

"Nothing."

"Should I let you be silent?"

"I don't know. Why don't you ask me some questions."

"You said you were searching for a therapist?"

"That's right."

"Can you tell me something about your past therapy experiences?"

"They were terrible."

"What do you mean, terrible?"

"Just what I said. Terrible."

"How many therapists have you had?"

"How many have I checked out? Or how many have I actually gone into therapy with?"

"Both."

"I've checked out hundreds. I've actually only been with three."

"How long were you with those three?"

"I was with the first one for nine years."

"When was that?"

"I started with him when I was 7, after my father died."

"Your father died when you were 7?"

"That's what I just said."

"It must have been traumatic for you if you began therapy then."

"It was my mother's idea, really. I never liked my father anyway."

"I see. How was your first therapist?"

"Abusive. All my therapists have been abusive."

"How were they abusive?"

"The first one was sexually abusive."

"What happened?"

He hesitated, probing me to see if he could trust me. "He used to masturbate me."

I envisioned Mr. Snickler as a tender, sulking boy, being masturbated by an aging therapist. "How'd that make you feel?"

"I enjoyed it at first. He said he was doing it to boost my spirits."

"Did it?"

"At first it did." He looked at me seductively, smiling mischievously and giving me a knowing look. An image of myself fondling Mr. Snickler flashed through my mind as he looked at me.

"And then?"

"Then I became disgusted. I felt betrayed." He sank down in his chair.

"Betrayed?"

"I don't want to talk about it. I haven't decided whether I want to be in therapy with you yet. I don't think you're going to be smart enough for me." He had sat up and was his surly self again.

"I see." I imagined myself zipping up Mr. Snickler, roughly. "So you're searching for a therapist who's smart enough for you."

"Smart enough and together enough. I find that most therapists aren't really together. Sooner or later they all disappoint me. I'm already disappointed in you, disappointed in your second book, disappointed in your trite shrink-type questions."

"I can be very disappointing and trite sometimes."

"Yes, you can."

The session went on in that tenor, circling around and around the same issues: Mr. Snickler's feelings that he was nothing, his feelings that all the therapists he had ever met were less than nothing, and his feelings that his mother was everything and nothing. At one point he made a remark about how all big-shot therapists were full of hot air, and I had a fantasy of one therapist after another being deflated by Mr. Snickler as he stuck pins into their sides: a man with a Freudian goatee, chuckling arrogantly, shriveling up as he chuckled; a woman with huge breasts pontificating about bad breasts (Klein 1932), then flattening and flitting around as the air leaked out of her; a white-haired, happy-faced Kohutian figure, bubbling with empathy, then flying into the air and whipping about the room as he slowly deflated.

At the end of the session I asked him what he

wanted to do. He paused and said, "I'd like to try another session. I still haven't made up my mind about you. Do you have an opening tomorrow?" I said I did. Then I asked him how he wanted to pay. "Just send a bill to my mother," he replied, a bitter smile at the edges of his lips. "Don't worry, you'll get your money."

I thought of him the rest of the day and I thought of him that night. I dreamed about him while I slept and I fretted over him as I ate breakfast. Mr. Snickler had gotten, as the saying goes, "under my skin."

There was a low-level feeling of dread about seeing him again, the kind of dread you feel when you know that somebody wants to murder you but he has not said anything about it, and you have not said anything about it, and he may not even know it himself. I knew he wanted to murder me, psychologically, and I had an idea about how he would try to do it, based on what had happened so far. What I could not gauge was to what extent he would go in achieving his aim.

I also knew that since he wanted to murder me, he himself must have felt psychologically murdered in the past. Shengold (1979) wrote about the kind of murder that happens through "man's inhumanity to man"—generally to children in their earliest years—dubbing it "soul murder." It can happen in many different ways: through sexual or physical abuse, through psychological oppression, through parental neglect or spoiling. The primary ingredient of soul murder is that "the victim is robbed of his identity and of the ability to maintain authentic feelings. Soul murder remains effective if the capacity to think and to know has been sufficiently interfered with—by way of brainwashing" (p. 557). Shengold added that the need to maintain the illusion of a good parent reinforces the defense mechanism of denial, so that the victim's "brainwashing" in turn becomes self-enforced. Others have reiterated this theme in different terminology (Ferenczi 1933, Laing 1971, Miller 1984, Seinfield 1990).

Soul-murdered persons are in some respects zombies—yes, like the zombies who appear in horror movies, rising out of their graves to take revenge on all the living; they are humans who are emotionally dead. They are jealous of the living and wish to pass along what was done to them in their childhood, to murder the souls of those around them who are able to do what they cannot do. Mr. Snickler saw me as one of the living. I was a man of achievement, I had written books, I had patients who admired me, and a life with friends and family. Mr. Snickler was a zombie with a mother who was no doubt keeping him in a state of living death (impotent dependency), a man with intellectual gifts he was unable to use, emotions he dared not directly express, and a sexual appetite he could not satisfy.

I understood from the kinds of fantasies that I was having about Mr. Snickler and his mother what kinds of things Mr. Snickler was projecting onto me. I understood that from the moment he walked into my office and even before, we had become locked in a life-and-death struggle in which resistance and counterresistance had immediately come to the fore. Because of my writings, he had already identified me as a misogynistic (mother-hating) sexist, a fiend with incestuous father cravings, and an intellectual upstart who uses his writing and his power as a therapist to exploit mothers and sons for his own narcissistic needs. This projective identification was in actuality the disowned aspects of himself, the split-off feelings, thoughts, and impulses that left him a zombie. It was actually he who harbored antifeminist views and a disgust for everything his feminist mother stood for (this would come out later), he who was smitten with incestuous impulses toward his mother and toward men who represented his father, he who was an intellectual upstart with grandiose narcissistic aspirations and oedipal envy. He warded off awareness of this disowned self through reaction formation (he was a staunch supporter of feminism), denial, splitting, and projective identification. However, so successful were his intimidation tactics and his disowning of these thoughts, feelings, and impulses, so skilled was he at projecting and identifying them as belonging to me, that I found myself having fantasies of conquering his mother sexually, of flattening him intellectually, and of fondling him incestuously. I also began to feel guilty about my writings and to wonder about the extent of my own narcissistic grandiosity.

I was well aware that my writings about feminism in both of the books mentioned by Mr. Snickler (1989, 1991a) were controversial. I now became aware of how those writings represented a cultural resistance on my part, and perhaps a characterological resistance as well. I had reacted angrily to what I saw as the excesses of the feminist movement, and though I tried to eliminate traces of that anger in my writing, it leaked through anyway. There was also some characterological anger there, stemming from masculine identification and the sense that men were not being treated fairly by feminists—which, in turn, went back to a deeper injury caused by my mother and father, the feeling that my mother had not treated men (me, my father) fairly.

In other words, Mr. Snickler, in reading my writings on feminism, felt that my resistance was not only directed at feminism but at his mother as well. Hence, through identification with the aggressor, he felt that I was resistant to him. He therefore formed a resistance to my cultural and characterological resistance (which then transformed my resistance into a counterresistance to his resistance) before he even entered my office. Once he stepped in, the battle lines were drawn. (It is for this reason that many, if not most, therapists are hesitant about revealing information about themselves and insist on being a blank screen.)

Between his first and second visits I tried to make sense out of Mr. Snickler's transference and resistance by putting together the pieces of information that he had given me. What had happened in his childhood? I knew only that his father had died when he was about 7 years old; that his relationship with his father was not very good; that he had started therapy with a male therapist at that time and had experienced sexual abuse at his hands; and that he had lived with, had his back scrubbed and been supported by his mother ever since. I speculated from this information that his mother was a controlling person who had never allowed her son to separate. She had probably been indulgent and pampering, stifling his development of mature ego skills, and interfering with his relationship with his father by having an emotionally incestuous relationship with him. Since he himself had mentioned the Oedipus complex, I saw this as an admission that he did suffer from it (the line from Hamlet, "Methinks the lady doth protest too much," comes to mind). I further speculated that his father was very much like himself, a glum, hostile man with his own oral, narcissistic rage and Oedipus complex, who tried to murder his son psychologically, reinforcing his fears of castration and his incestuous and dependent attachment to his mother.

When the father died, the boy's unconscious desire to kill his father and take his mother for himself would have been realized. This would have reinforced his passive-homosexual feelings (the desire to give himself to other men sexually as an appeasement for having won the mother away from the father). It would have also reinforced his oedipal guilt and his fear of retaliation by other father figures (zombie-fathers back from the dead): hence, his repeating pattern when meeting surrogate fathers would consist of a defensive posture of killing or being killed. In this way of perceiving things, people lived off other people's blood; one person's happiness was at the expense of another's unhappiness; one person's pleasure at the expense of another's pain; one person's life at the expense of another's death.

When his first therapist masturbated him at the age of 7, he was probably responding to impulses that the boy induced in him, just as Mr. Snickler had induced them in me. Mr. Snickler wanted either to seduce and give himself sexually to (and thereby be soul-murdered by) the therapist or to attack, degrade, and otherwise soul-murder and dump the therapist (as his mother had done to him). Apparently Mr. Snickler's search for a therapist—he said he had "checked out" hundreds—was in reality not so much a search mission as it was a search-and-destroy mission. And I was next on his list.

I did not want to die, so I waited in dread for his next visit the following afternoon. I thought about canceling the session, stalling for time. I thought about telling him that I had decided not to work with him. I did neither, seemingly paralyzed by fear. He arrived a few minutes late and looked even more surly than he had the day before.

"Would you like to try lying down today?" I asked. I wanted to get his eyes away from me.

"I haven't decided yet whether or not I want to be a patient."

"Well, while you're deciding, how about lying down."

"Why should I?"

"It helps put the therapy on a deeper framework."

"I don't know if I want to be on a deeper framework."

I shrugged my shoulders. "Okay."

"You want me to lie down on the couch? Fine, I'll lie down on the couch."

He lay down stiffly, his head half turned toward me.

"How does it feel?" I asked.

"It doesn't feel any different than sitting up. It makes me feel a little sick to my stomach, actually."

"You feel nauseous?"

"The word is *nauseated*, not *nauseous*. Yes, that's what I just said."

My fingers began tapping on my thigh. "You don't have to lie down if it makes you sick."

"I'll be all right."

At that moment the phone rang and I answered it as is my custom. When I hung up he half turned to me again.

"Would you mind not answering the phone during my session?"

"Suppose there's an emergency and somebody needs me?"

"I'm paying for this session, and I don't want you answering the phone during my session. It's infuriating."

"So if somebody calls and is suicidal, I should just let him go through with it?"

"How many suicidal patients do you have?"

"Three," I lied.

"Well, they can just wait until my session is over."

I did not answer. There was a silence. One could hear a commercial jingle playing on the radio in the waiting room.

"Could you turn that radio down?"

"If you want to turn it down, go ahead."

He jumped up from the couch, yanked open the door, and reached out into the waiting room to turn it down. When he returned he said, "I don't know why you have your radio on WQXR." He shook his head contemptuously.

"Why not?"

"Haven't you ever heard of WNCN? WNCN has better music and no commercials." My fingers tapped faster. "So, what should I talk about?"

"Whatever comes into your head."

"I suppose I should talk about my mother. Isn't that the thing to do—bash mothers?" He proceeded to talk about his mother, elliptically, approaching and avoiding his feelings about her. He spoke with great difficulty about loving her and hating her, about financially exploiting her and feeling guilty about it, about problems with relationships and problems with therapists. "Are you going to say something?" he suddenly asked.

"What did you want me to say?"

"Anything. I'm not paying you to sit there and say nothing."

"What should I say?"

"You're the shrink. Ask me a question."

"You said you hated your mother sometimes. Why?"

"That's a stupid question. And predictable, coming from you."

"What do you mean?"

"Predictable after reading your book. I reread the section about feminism again last night, and it really is quite vulgar. It's obvious you know nothing about where feminism is now, about the third wave. Your criticism is all about feminists who lived years ago. My mother refers to men like you as paleopigs. Naturally you want to know all about my hatred of my mother. You're obviously full of hatred for women and probably for your mother as well."

"If you see me as a woman-hater, what does that mean in terms of your therapy with me?"

"Oh, God, will you stop with the dime-store analysis."

"I seem to be annoying you."

"You're annoying the hell out of me. There's something insipid about your questions. Something childish, babyish, idiotic." He waited for a response. "Well, are you going to say anything?"

"What should I say?"

"*What should I say*?" he mimicked me in a baby voice, then rose up on his hands, whirled around, and glared at me. "You really are insipid. In fact, you're worse than insipid. You're fetal. There's something absolutely fetal about you."

He lay back grinning.

I sat in my chair, momentarily stunned. My soul had taken a beating, I was sure, and was probably flying about the room like some fragile butterfly trying to escape inevitable doom. I felt that the breath of life had been knocked out of me and that rigor mortis had set in. Looking at the delighted grin on his face and at the glee in his countenance made me feel even gloomier. I thought of the scene from the movie *The Exorcist,* when the priest becomes infected by the demons that have been possessing the girl and heaves

himself out of the window. Mr. Snickler was possessed too, I thought, but not by demons. He was
possessed by rage, narcissistic, sadomasochistic,
and borderline rage that spilled from his every
word and glance and had now been spewed on me.

As I sat there I imagined myself jerking Mr.
Snickler up from the couch and heaving him out
the window, or at least out the door, and maybe
giving him a few kicks in the behind for good
measure. In fact, I had this irrational fear that if I
did not kick him out instantly either he or I would
kill each other. Then I thought: yes, that must have
been how it was in the oedipal days before Mr.
Snickler's father died. There must have been a
mighty life-or-death struggle between Mr. Snickler
and his father, and Mr. Snickler must have en-
dured in a state of terror. This was the repeating
pattern that got re-created in each of his therapy
experiences, I thought.

It was Eros and Thanatos being played out in
the resistance and counterresistance. His remark
that there was something fetal about me harked
back to Freud's death instinct theory, wherein he
posited in humans a drive to return to the womb
and to death, particularly when the forces of life
(Eros) are blighted, and noted that "during the oral
stage of organization of the libido, the act of obtaining erotic mastery over an object coincides
with that object's destruction" (1920, p. 95).
Anyone who has observed how infants and tod-
dlers chew away at, stomp on, and in other ways
obliterate their toys, and any mother who has had
her breast bitten by a teething infant, understands
what Freud means here.

It was not just an oedipal drama going on between Mr. Snickler and me, but rather an oedipal drama on top of an oral and anal drama. One drama was of oedipal rivalry and envy, having to do with taking and protecting Mom and destroying Dad and Dad's achievements; one was about anal dominance and submission—either he would control and degrade me or I would control and degrade him; and one was about oral sadism, dependency, and narcissism. At the oral core of this three-layered drama was the fear of reengulfment by the witch-mother of primitive oral fantasies. Mr. Snickler's fear of reengulfment had been projected onto me with other disowned aspects. I, not he, was the vulnerable fetus who was in danger of reengulfment.

At this level we were also caught up in a battle about symbiotic merger. It seemed to me that Mr. Snickler was to some extent still fixated in the symbiotic stage, was still bound in that way to his mother, and was struggling against the same kind of merger with me. He either had to disavow me completely (engulf me), or give in to me completely (let me engulf him). Both again meant life or death. This of course is reminiscent of Searles's (1979) writings about the kinds of resistance and counterresistance that emerge during certain phases of working with schizophrenic patients. Namely, it brings to mind the intense involvement that Searles describes in working with schizophrenic patients, and the feelings of merger and the inability to distinguish what is self and what is the other. I do not believe that Mr. Snickler was schizophrenic per se, but he had a certain paranoid

schizophrenic underpinning to his character, manifested by this fear of being infantalized, against
which he defended by infantalizing others first.
Thus, I was drawn into this world of schizophrenic
merger, and it was as if a spell had been cast over
me and over my office. My office became a womb,
his mother's womb, in which Mr. Snickler and I
battled over who could be born and who had to
remain in an infantile-dependent state. The unofficial rules of this battle were, unfortunately, that
only one of us was allowed to leave the womb.
These were the unspoken rules somehow transmitted by his mother. This was the struggle he had
gone through with his father, which had ended in
his father being, symbolically, the sacrificial lamb.

As I pondered this, I found myself having
flashbacks to my own past. I saw my father, my
brothers, and my mother. I recalled the forces and
counterforces that had prevailed in my family and
felt the mixture of unsoothed and unresolved feelings still lurking within me. How often had I feared
my father, competed with my brothers, felt incestuous feelings toward my mother? How often had I
been in awe of my mother's private parts and
envious of her power of giving and nurturing life? I
realized that my countertransference feelings and
impulses were not all simply induced by Mr.
Snickler, but that some of them were in actuality
my transference to Mr. Snickler: He had become
my menacing father and teasing brothers, and his
mother had become my mother.

Had my own transference in turn induced this
particular response from Mr. Snickler? Did my own
unresolved fears about my father, mother, and

brothers, my passivity, my narcissism, my masochism, contribute to the interchange we were
having? Was I in fact acting "idiotic"and "babyish" and "fetal"? Had Mr. Snickler sniffed out my
own fear of/wish for punishment and destruction?
What comes first, the transference or the countertransference? Resistance or counterresistance?

I decided to play it safe and simply respond
from my feelings. "You asked if I'm going to say
anything," I said at last. "First of all, I'd like to say
that I feel very hurt by everything you've said. I am
human, you know, and I do bleed. Second, I'd like
to point out that I've treated you with respect since
you first contacted me, and I would like to be
treated with respect by you in return. You're certainly entitled to verbalize any thoughts you have,
but in an atmosphere of respect. I experience you
as being contemptuous and hostile, as wanting to
hurt me. I'm not here to be your whipping-father. If
that's your idea, then I think you may be in the
wrong place."

"That's the most normal thing any shrink has
ever said to me," he replied, smiling.

He came back the next day. Somehow I knew it
would be our last session. I did not dread this visit
as I had the previous session, but I was instead
resolutely looking forward to it. I had decided after
carrying Mr. Snickler with me again through the
night that most of the feelings I was having had
indeed been induced by him, and even if I had been
a totally healthy individual, without any emotional
freight from my own past, I would have been
affected by him. I also decided that he was asking

to be confronted, and I had developed several plans for confronting him if he attempted to attack me again.

However, when he strode into my office he had a calm expression on his face.

"I've decided to see another therapist," he said, sitting down in the chair.

"Good luck," I countered.

"Why do you say that?"

"Your negative feelings about me and about my writing are so strong that it would have been difficult to overcome them, and your way of expressing those feelings tended to wipe me out to such an extent that I couldn't reach you."

"You're probably right. Actually, the therapist I've decided to see, well, I wiped him out too. I think I was even more hostile with him than with you. But three weeks later he called me and asked me to come in for another session, and when I did he totally knocked me off my feet. He told me that he disagreed with everything I had said about him and then explained why he was the perfect therapist for me. When I left his office I was enraged, and it was the next day that I read your books and called you. I guess some of the anger you got was displaced from him."

"So it seems."

"I'm sorry about that," he said, rather glibly.

"I'm sorry too," I said, just as glibly.

There was a silence. Something was happening to his face, a subtle quiver of cheek muscles.

"So . . . do you hate me?" he asked. His tone had mellowed considerably. Now that he had "destroyed" me, he could allow himself to be merciful. For the first time I sensed that he saw the real me and the real relationship between us—that I was simply a professional who was human and was trying his best to help him, and that he had been rude and verbally abusive toward me. For the first time he cared about my feelings and was not dismissing me.

"Yes, I feel hate for you." As a matter of reality testing I wanted him to know what kinds of feelings he had induced, especially as he had asked.

"I can understand that," he quickly replied, and looked down.

"Why's that?"

"It's what generally happens."

"What feelings did you want me to feel?"

"Hate."

"I thought so."

"I want everybody to hate me."

"Yes."

"And everybody usually does sooner or later."

"What's that about?"

"Well, I'm not too good at getting people to love me, so getting them to hate me is the next best thing." He looked at me somewhat apologetically. "The bottom line is, I'm full of hate myself. I feel hateful, so I want to be hated. I'm full of hate for my mother, but I don't know what to do with it." He glanced up again, perhaps expecting an I-told-you-so response. "By the way, I was thinking about your criticism of feminism again last night. As odd as this may seem, there's actually a part of me that agrees with everything you said. In a way women do want it both ways, and feminism does feel like a

manipulation. I don't know how I feel about feminism. I don't know how I feel about my mother.
Sometimes I love her, and sometimes I'm disgusted
by her."

The muscles in his cheeks began to twitch and
he sat there still and silent for a few minutes before
some tears began to fall from his eyes. He struggled
mightily against the release of these tears, as if
their release signaled his defeat, like flying a white
flag. But out they came, these locked up tears, and
then he began rocking back and forth. After a time
his face grew dark and his eyes squinty, and he
blurted out, "I hate that bitch, I hate her! I'm not
supposed to hate her. It's wrong to hate her, but I
hate her! There, are you satisfied? I hate my
mother! Are you satisfied?" He broke into sobs and
continued to sob for a few minutes before he again
got control of himself.

We both sat in silence until the session was
over. I arose, and he arose and shook my hand.

"You know," he said, with small, reddened
eyes. "If I hadn't already signed on with this other
therapist, it might have worked out with you after
all."

"It might have. Anyway, I wish you good luck
with this therapist. He sounds as if he's on the right
track."

"Maybe."

"And if it doesn't work out, you can always call
me."

"Thanks."

He stood for a moment squinting at me. I was
in front of the window, and the afternoon sun
glimmered across his face. He looked at me with

what I thought was bitterness becoming astonishment, becoming longing, becoming gratitude, becoming fear.

I never heard from him again, and that did not bother me. Mr. Snickler managed to leave a "stinger" in my psyche, as difficult patients often do. Even today when I receive a phone call from somebody who says that he or she has just read one of my books and adores it, my blood jumps just a little, my shoulders rise imperceptably, and I have to calm myself for a moment before answering, "That's nice."

---

# 11

# Emotional Contagion

My treatment of Mr. Snickler brings up a related consideration. Often while working with this difficult borderline patient—as well as with other patients with similar character structures—I found myself besieged with feelings, thoughts, and impulses that I would not ordinarily have had. My emotions had become infected by Mr. Snickler's emotions, and my state of mind by his state of mind. Hence, my countertransference and counterresistance were fueled by this emotional contagion, and I suspect that that is often, if not usually, the case. There appears to be some basic connection between counterresistance and emotional contagion.

I alluded in the previous chapter to the movie *The Exorcist*, in which a Catholic priest attempted to exorcise the demons from an adolescent girl, utilizing ancient rituals of the Church, only to find that he had caught her demons himself. This is precisely how emotional contagion often feels, especially when it involves negative, unwanted feelings—as if you were possessed.

Are emotional states, like viruses, catching? That they are is a readily acknowledged fact; one can find numerous instances of how fear, anger, laughter, and tears are infectious. However, what is not readily acknowledged is the extent to which emotions are transmitted from person to person or from group to group in our daily lives, and how such transmissions not only affect our feeling state but also our thoughts, attitudes, and personalities. At times, emotional contagion can have positive results, as when a leader's optimism and good cheer fill all his followers with the same spirit. At other times it can have negative results, as when a mother who is angry with her husband unconsciously transmits that anger to her infant, roughly picking him up, glaring at him, causing him to cry out in discomfort.

Deliberate emotional contagion is used by various practitioners to influence, control, or destroy individuals or groups. It has been described in various ways and by various terms—voodoo, witchcraft, sorcery, hypnosis, psychology, mind control, projective identification, black magic—and has been around from ancient times to the present. However, many if not most people remain unconscious of the emotions or behavior they induce in others, or the emotions and behavior that are being induced in themselves. This fact has been verified by psychoanalysts who encounter emotional contagion (or emotional induction) every day in their work. Conscious and unconscious contagion occurs in the most respectable homes, institutions, and societies, and is often at the root of our most popular values, ideologies, religions, and political causes. It also plays a role in the development of mental illness, criminality, and physical disease, as well as in the instigation of prejudice and war.

When I was in caught up in a life-and-death, resistance–counterresistance struggle with Mr. Snickler, I also felt possessed. I felt as if there were demons inside of me, felt my very cells buzzing with rage, as though some fiend had gotten inside me. This experience with Mr. Snickler and others made me curious about emotional contagion and its relation to counterresistance.

## HISTORICAL PERSPECTIVE
## OF EMOTIONAL CONTAGION

Emotional contagion has been around since ancient times. Often it has been viewed as synonymous with the "forces of darkness," which are at various times attributed to Satan, the stars, sexual perversity, or supernatural events. These dark forces were purportedly used by witches, warlocks, shamans, and sorcerers to perform evil and magic deeds, such as casting spells on lovers, getting "under the skin," putting on a hex, controlling the mind, conquering the spirit, and torturing people to death or insanity.

References to witchcraft go back to the beginnings of history, as do injunctions against it. The

Babylonian king Hammurabi prohibited it in his Code, and there was also an injunction against it in the Bible: "Thou shall not suffer a witch to live" (Exodus 22:18). When Christianity became entrenched as the official religion of Europe, all who defied it became known as witches; indeed, the Roman Catholic Church treated secularism as heresy and identified heresy with witchcraft.

One of the most striking examples of emotional contagion on a mass scale was the witch-hunting mania that obsessed Europe from the eleventh to the eighteenth centuries, during which time from 300,000 to 9,000,000 witches were burned at the stake, usually naked, with their backs turned to their executioners, so that they could not flash their evil eye, which was thought to kill at a glance. During this period all mental ailments were attributed to an individual's being in league with the Devil. Witches were blamed for every disorder or catastrophe, from epidemics, to droughts, to floods, to earthquakes. They were said to cause men to become impotent and women sterile. Witches were said to cut off and collect male genitals, keeping them in birds' nests (Roback and Kiernan 1969).

Superstitions from these times illustrate a belief in, and fear of, emotional contagion. For example, according to one superstition, if a mandrake shrieked when pulled from the earth, anyone who heard the shriek was said to go mad. To ward off possession by evil spirits, people relied on magical potions and incantations. One prescription for warding off evil spirits called for the testicle of a goat, which was killed on a Tuesday at midnight during the first quarter of the moon, and the heart of a dog, mixed with the feces of a newborn baby.

The notorious *Malleus Maleficarum* (the bible of witch-hunting written in 1484), cites a tale of a witch who enticed four abbots, one at a time, into her boudoir. She put them under a spell, had sex with them, fed them dung, and smiled at them wantonly as she sent them on their way. Afterward three died and the fourth "lost his senses" (Roback and Kiernan, 1969).

Witches were not the only ones to make use of emotional contagion. The shamans of primitive tribes also frequently did so. For example, Chagnon (1968) describes a tribe called the Yana-mamö, the fiercest tribe of the jungles of Brazil. According to Yanamamö mythology, children were the primary targets of sorcery by other tribes, who tried to magically attack and devour the vulnerable parts of the children's souls, while sorcerers of the Yanomamö tried to do the same with regard to children of other tribes. Such myths, told to children repeatedly, served to terrorize them and induce greater fierceness.

Benedict (1934) writes of how primitive societies, through their medicine men, placated evil forces often through the sacrificial death of a virgin. She describes the fear and antagonism that were commonly shown toward medicine men, who were depended on to cure the sick, make rain, assure the success of a hunt and of war, exorcise demons, smell out evil, and denounce evil-doers and bring them to ruin. "He had the power to harm more particularly than he had power to help. Their attitude toward him was compounded of fear, of hatred, and of suspicion. His death could not be avenged, and if he failed in his cures and suspicion came to rest upon him, he was commonly killed" (p. 113)

Greek mythology is replete with stories that allude to the process of emotional contagion. There were, for instance, the sirens—evil creatures—who lived on a rocky island, singing in deceptively beautiful voices that were capable of luring sailors to shipwreck and death. And there was Circe, a powerful sorceress who turned people who looked at her into swine.

As humans became more civilized, witches and shamans were replaced by priests and doctors. Estabrooks (1943) points out how various societies made use of hypnosis as a way of driving away evil or to induce behavior. For example, the ancient Greeks had sleep temples, to which sufferers of emotional problems would come and be induced into a trance by a priest, during which trance they "would be visited by the various gods who were the patron saints of medicine" (p. 123); presumably these gods included Hypnos, the Greek god of sleep. A few centuries later, during the late 1700s, Franz Anton Mesmer went throughout Europe "mesmerizing" hysterics, giving them suggestions, and curing them by utilizing a force he called "animal magnetism."

The proverb, "All's fair in love and war," hints at the sorcery or trickery that is often a part of both romantic relations and violent conflicts such as war. Lovers of all ages and from all levels of society have sought the advice and aid of witches, sorcerers, and shamans in influencing the behavior of a loved one or in getting revenge against those who have spurned them. St. Valentine's Day represents a modern-day ritual going back to the Roman Empire, when the festival of the Lupercalia was celebrated every February 15th in order to invoke from the gods greater virility. The god of love, Cupid—often depicted in paintings as a chubby cherub with a bow and arrow—came to symbolize passion and virility, and was said to induce these in a mortal by shooting one of his arrows into the individual. Words such as *seduce, enchant, fascinate, entice, entrance, bewitch,* and *captivate,* are allusions to the emotional induction that often takes place in romantic relationships.

Advertisers on television and other media attempt to induce consumers to buy their products by using seduction (beautiful women often do the selling), enchantment, and hypnotic techniques. Politicians try to induce voters to vote for them, and to ignite a flame of emotional contagion. Countries at war try to arouse an emotional state of patriotism and a feverish hatred of the enemy, while attempting to invoke a response of terror in the enemy.

Religious crusades and mass movements are pointed examples of emotional contagion. Under the influence of religious fervor numerous wars have been fought and millions have been burned at the stake. One of the more bizarre examples of religious contagion happened in our own era, when Jim Jones, a womanizing minister of an offbeat church in California, took about 900 followers to Guyana, South America, where he led them in the largest mass suicide ritual in recorded history.

Political and cultural movements such as the Nazi movement in Germany, the communist movement in Russia and China, and the "hippie" movement in America in the 1960s, were all fueled by emotional contagion, as was the panic that led to the stock market crash in 1929 and the mass suicide and depression that followed.

Finally, the family is a significant, if not the original, breeding ground of emotional contagion. Parents routinely induce emotions and behaviors in their children, most often unconsciously. Laing (1971) referred to emotional contagion in families as a kind of hypnotic induction. When emotional induction and contagion are overwhelming, and when they are combined with negative suggestion or other environmental impingements, they can lead to neurotic, narcissistic, sociopathic, perverse, or psychotic character formation.

## THEORIES OF EMOTIONAL CONTAGION

The early literature of psychiatry contains many references to emotional contagion related to personality disorders. Often an individual suffering from severe hysteria or paranoia would infect a spouse or child, inducing similar behavior, and the term *folie à deux* was coined to describe this condition. Flournay (1927) reported a case involving a woman who infected her half brother with her paranoid belief that her former employer was out to destroy them both. They kept the shutters and doors of their house shut tight for many months. Only when the boy was on the verge of death from hunger and cold did the woman realize what she was doing. Flournay, in examining the boy, noted that he did not have the intense tone of an authentic delusional person, as had his half sister; rather, his state represented "no more than a particular case of general suggestibility" (p. 54).

A social psychologist, McDougall (1920) studied the impact of the spread of emotions on group behavior. He was one of the first to notice that emotions such as hysteria affect not only the mood of the masses, but thoughts and behavior as well. The pioneer of character analysis, Reich (1933), also examined mass emotional contagion, and invented the term "the emotional plague" to describe its sinister repercussions. Reich posited the existence of "plague characters," individuals susceptible to emotional plague reactions, and noted that such characters formed the core of all mass movements and were extremely resistant to reasoning or therapy.

In behavioral psychology, Milgram's (1974) experiments concerning obedience to authority described earlier, demonstrated that when an authority (in this case a Yale University scientist) instructs selected individuals to push buttons administering electric shocks to human subjects, 62 percent of such individuals will push those buttons, ignoring the screams of "victims." The authority figures in these experiments induced a mood of calm obedience and a kind of sanctified sadism such as that found in the Nazi death camps in Germany during World War II.

Estabrooks (1943), a psychologist and clinical hypnotist, studied the relationship of hypnosis to emotion. He asserts that "it is highly probable that hypnotism in its turn depends on emotion" (p. 137), adding that suggestion depends on transference, which Estabrooks sees as an emotional state. In other words, hypnotism is another name for emotional contagion, and perhaps its prototype. To illustrate the link between suggestion and emotion, he cites an example in which he gave a hypnotic suggestion that went awry. He suggested to Mr. Smith, while he was hypnotized, that when he awoke he would want to sit in Mr. Brown's chair. Upon awaking, Mr. Smith demanded Mr. Brown's chair. When Mr. Brown refused to give it up, Mr. Smith picked up Mr. Brown and hurled him across the room. After taking his seat, he savagely warned that if Mr. Brown so much as opened his mouth he would throw him out of the window as well. Somehow, through transference, Estabrook's suggestion to Mr. Smith became converted into permission to become a violent bully (a kind of replication of Milgram's experiments). The suggestion somehow aroused a transference reaction toward Mr. Brown and a delayed expression of emotional contagion. Probably Mr. Smith had once been infected by a parent or sibling and had been forced to repress the emotion, which, upon his being hypnotized by Estabrooks, was set into motion as a posthypnotic suggestion and acted out toward Mr. Brown. The transference was representative of the parent or sibling who had originally engendered Mr. Smith's anger.

Indeed, Estabrooks sees a parallel between what he calls the "Freudian complex" and the posthypnotic suggestion. For example, a child is frightened by a cat; later in life he develops a cat phobia. The original fright was a form of hypnotic induction (emotional contagion), and the cat phobia represents the activation of the implied posthypnotic suggestion (beware of cats). If such an individual with a fear of cats meets up with a formal or informal hypnotist who suggests that cats are a menace and he should protect the public from them, the man will probably respond by becoming a mass killer of cats. According to Estabrooks, people often hypnotize each other without knowing it.

In psychoanalysis the phenomenon of emotional contagion was at first linked with the concept of projective identification. Klein (1932) invented the term *projective identification* to describe the fantasies of infants. Children in the first months of life, she asserts, tend to have omnipotent fantasies that unwanted parts of the personality (sexual or aggressive impulses) are in actuality located in another object (the mother); thus, they perceive the mother as an all-powerful witch who wants to destroy them. Other analysts have since provided a thorough explanation of how not only children project and identify parts of themselves onto parents, but how parents do likewise with children (as when a mother decides that a certain child is evil, just as her older brother was evil, and treats the child accordingly), and patients do likewise with therapists. A patient may be distantly aware of wanting to deceive or cheat his therapist; he projectively identifies the therapist as a potential con artist and treats the therapist as though he were going to try to con him at any moment, glancing at him warily during sessions, withholding information, laughing sarcastically at attempts by the therapist to reach a level of honest communication with him. By treating the therapist in this way, he may induce such characteristics and their associated emotions in the analyst, who may find himself behaving deceitfully, or having thoughts of doing so. In effect, the therapist has become infected. If the therapist has not had enough training and begins to act out the role with which he has been projectively identified—that is, act out his countertransference—he will unwittingly repeat a pathogenic situation from the patient's past rather than resolve it.

Projective identification also occurs in everyday life. For example, those deemed as "possessed" by the Catholic Church in earlier times were generally the victims of the projective identifications of priests, who split off the evil characteristics in themselves and projected them onto "heathens." A paranoid husband may projectively identify his wife as an unfaithful "slut," and she, responding to being treated as though she were, may actually begin having affairs.

The first psychoanalyst to use the term *emotional contagion* was Escalona (1953). In her research on emotional development during infancy, she used it to describe one of the two ways mothers transmit their feelings, purposes, and intentions. Consciously, she pointed out, mothers communicate verbally with their infants; unconsciously they infect them with nonverbal language. As an example of contagion she noted that when an anxious person holds a baby, the baby cries, even though it may have just been fed; when a calm person holds the same baby, it will stop crying. Thus, an excited or worried mother, out of touch with her feelings, will attempt to calm and reassure her baby by hugging or rocking the child in her arms, but without success. Escalona was not sure how this contagion worked, but asserted that it took place not only between mothers and infants, but also between therapists and patients, and between lovers. She described how it occurs in ordinary situations, such as when one does not like the atmosphere in a store or at a party, and chooses not to enter that store or engage in conversation at the party. She also noted that some infants, and some people, seem to have a particular susceptibility to emotional contagion.

Though he did not refer to emotional contagion directly, Winnicott alludes to it in his work. For example, he describes (1965) how a mother's depression affected her son. This mother was ill treated by her husband, causing her to be chronically depressed. Her depression, a defense against arousal of anger and violence in her, was transmitted to her son. The boy stopped eating and developed diabetes. Winnicott describes how the mother brought the boy to his clinic, worried about the boy's state but quite unaware of her own depression and its effect on the boy. He did not attempt to treat the mother, knowing she would be resistant, but instead dealt with the boy's symptoms. "Naturally, the boy besides being treated for his diabetes was given help in regard to the understanding of the home situation. I am not surprised, however, to find that what I do does not clear up the bigger problem, which is the mother's chronic depression" (p. 53).

More recently psychoanalysts have begun to study the emotional climate of the therapy office. Winnicott (1965) wrote of the feelings that were induced in therapists by depressed, antisocial, or psychotic patients, observing in particular how patients can induce hate in their therapists. Brill (1949) pointed to the emotionality of the transference and asserted, "Of course, emotions beget emotions" (p. 224). Rado (1953) referred to emotional neutralization that was necessary for the therapist to resolve the "contagiousness of emotions" (p. 266).

Searles (1979) wrote of a psychotic woman who was so fragmented that she induced in the entire hospital staff a feeling of unreality. He himself experienced "a quite terrible feeling of unrelatedness" (p. 203) that made him think at times he was talking to an extraterrestrial. At other times the same patient evoked violent emotions, so that he felt "so threatened and enraged that I was seriously afraid lest I lose control of my own murderous feelings, and kill her" (p. 199).

In his work with Miss B., Kernberg (Kernberg et al., 1989) illustrates how a patient aroused a succession of feelings and attitudes in him, and how he handled it. This patient, an intellectual young woman, had striven for months to get an appointment with him, but once she had gotten it she began to disparage him. In one session, she smiled apologetically and said she did not want to hurt him, but she agreed with her mother's assessment of him: he was provincial, lacked self-assurance, did not possess intellectual depth, and probably would not be able to tolerate her being really open with him. She said all this in a friendly way, and it took Kernberg a while to realize that the underlying tone was condescension. He began to feel dejected, to experience hopelessness about the therapy working out, to harbor impulses of giving up. Then he realized that he was feeling and acting just as the patient had suggested, when she told him he was incapable of intellectual depth or of tolerating her being open with him. Eventually he was able to use these induced feelings to understand her. He recognized that she had identified with her mother and that her attitudes toward him contained a projective identification—unconsciously she wanted to induce in Kernberg a feeling of low self-esteem and hopelessness so that she would be off the hook. "It's he who's inferior, not me," she could tell herself. Kernberg also understood that Miss B. was frightened of him and that "there was an act of revenge in the patient's devaluation, the counterpart of her sense in the past that he would assert his superiority and devalue her" (p. 96).

Emotional induction in therapy, and its relation to ego formation, was also studied extensively by Spotnitz. "If human beings are capable of influencing each other's emotional states, and emotional states influence human behavior, then the factor of emotional induction becomes an important one for scientific consideration," he asserts (Spotnitz and Meadow 1976, p. 75). Like Escalona, Spotnitz cannot explain the process entirely, but he notes that the more narcissistic most patients

are, the more intense are the feelings they induce
in therapists. He also points out that those therapists who are most susceptible to acting out induced feelings (subjective countertransference) are
those who have not resolved issues from their own
pasts. "Whereas subjective countertransference is
altered in some way by atypical tendencies in the
analyst, objective countertransference is the predictable response of the emotionally mature ob-
server" (p. 84). In other words, Spotnitz believes
we are all susceptible to induced feelings, but those
of us who are emotionally mature will be able to
objectify induced feelings and not act on them
rashly. Emotional induction is a reciprocal process:
a patient's intense transference feelings induce a
correspondingly intense countertransference response.

Seinfeld (1990), although he did not write
about emotional contagion per se, nevertheless
convincingly describes the "bad objects" that have
been internalized by patients and then transferred
onto the therapist. He speaks of how these internalized bad objects (representations of split-off, toxic
aspects of primary figures in patients' childhoods)
come to haunt the therapy treatment and to lead to
negative therapeutic reactions and a type of countertransference characterized by an ambivalent
symbiotic quality.

## EMOTIONAL CONTAGION
## AND COUNTERRESISTANCE

There is probably a scientific explanation for emotional contagion and its relation to counterresist-

ance. However, as yet nobody has come up with one that is adequate. The following may be said, descriptively, about emotional contagion:

1. It refers to a process in which one object, upon coming into contact with one or more other objects, induces a state of overwhelming arousal (emotional excitement) which, when combined with an implied or actual suggestion, leads to a change in thought, behavior, mood, attitude, or character. This emotional excitement corresponds physiologically with the the arousal of the sympathetic nervous system and the discharge of adrenalin and other chemicals into the blood, as well as with increased hormonal activity.

2. Primary emotional contagion refers to the original contagion between a mother or other caretaker and an infant. This contagion can sometimes begin in utero. Secondary emotional contagion is induced, and suffered by those who have already experienced a primary emotional contagion, which seems to render them susceptible to catching certain emotional states and frames of mind from others.

3. It differs from psychic trauma, although it can be an aspect of it. Emotional contagion seems to occur in connection with traumatic events.

4. It always occurs between a sender, who is in some way contagious, and a receiver, who is in some way susceptible. Whether

one is a sender or receiver depends on the particular circumstances and one's character structure and past experiences.

5. Objective emotional contagion is related to conscious, constructive forms, as when a teacher tries to infect his students with a spirit of well-being. Subjective emotional contagion is related to unconscious and destructive forms.

6. The prototype of emotional contagion may be hypnosis.

From an ego-psychology standpoint, emotional contagion represents a flooding of the ego with more excitement than it can master or discharge, rendering it weak and susceptible to influence. In the language of behavioral psychology, it would be described as the transmission by one object, in a state of arousal, of an aversive stimulus to another object, which does not expect such a stimulus or is unable to handle its intensity. In order to escape the aversive stimulus, the second object must learn a new behavior (a conditioned response) in relation to this particular kind of aversive stimulus.

Looking at this from the perspective of therapy, it appears that the degree of a therapist's subjective counterresistance is related to the degree of emotional contagion between the patient and therapist. The less a patient is able to verbalize his or her thoughts and feelings directly, the more emotionally contagious he or she will be. And the degree to which a therapist is susceptible to emotional contagion depends on his or her own level of emotional maturity and ego-strength—that is, on the severity of the fixations that have weakened the ego because of past traumas involving similar emotional contagion.

An incident that occurred to a patient a while back illustrates what I mean. The patient, a rather shy young man, went to a movie with his girlfriend. Another couple sat down beside them, and the woman of this couple, who was next to him, began giving him the eye. He would be watching the movie and feel somebody looking at him. He would turn away and find her staring at him "coldly, like she despised me." He quickly looked away and tried to ignore her, but he felt pulses of fear inside him and his body stiffened. A few minutes later he felt her foot on top of his. He reflexively moved his foot away and thought nothing of it. Then he felt it again. This time she put her foot, which was adorned with a leather shoe, on top of the toe of his shoe, which was also made of leather. She pressed down hard and kept her foot there. He looked at her but she was watching the movie and pretending not to notice what she was doing with her foot. For a moment he doubted his senses. He looked down at the floor and saw that, yes, her foot was on his. He tried to move his foot away, but found that his leg was paralyzed. He could not move it at all. Then a wave of excitement such as he had never experienced before shot right up to his crotch. Within a few seconds he had become erect and then ejaculated. The woman seemed to sense what had happened. She slowly and triumphantly slid her foot away, glared at him once more, and continued to watch the movie, holding hands with her male companion. My patient, naturally, was shattered. He sat dumbfounded for the remainder of the movie. He wanted to say something to the woman, but she and her companion left before the movie ended.

When my patient told me this story, I found myself getting excited. Perhaps as you read this you too are experiencing some excitement. He had been infected by this woman, and had thus become contagious himself and was transmitting his excitement to me. Now I am transmitting it to you. Thus our words, our behavior, transmit not only ideas but also emotions. And since emotions affect thinking and attitude, emotional contagion can influence one's personality.

The woman in the theater had, through a cold stare and a touch of her foot, rendered him as helpless as a child. In seconds she had overpowered him, psychologically, shattering his sense of himself. He was in a daze all that weekend and still slightly in a daze when he came to my office. How had she been able to do it? My patient had had a tyrannical mother who had disparaged his sexuality. One of his most common sexual fantasies was about a witch ordering him to masturbate. Hence, the experience with this woman in the theater activated all the fear and excitement connected with this fantasy and with the repressed feelings about his tyrannical mother. His mother's tyranny and disparaging attitude had been the primary emotional contagion; this was the secondary one.

Each of us has an emotional field. We read one another's emotional fields and respond to them rather than to the content of our language. To the extent that we are not in touch with our feelings, our language is composed of rationalizations, denials, and deceptions to hide our feelings. The woman in the theater felt the man's emotional field and knew that she could have that kind of perverse power over him, knew that he was susceptible to this kind of emotional contagion, even though the manner he presented was of someone rather prim and proper. Perhaps he reminded her of a younger brother of whom she was jealous. He transferred his mother onto her, and she transferred her younger brother onto him. She was resistant to him, resistant to allowing him to watch the movie in peace. He developed a counterresistance, wanting to get away from her. His counterresistance made him all the more susceptible to contamination. That which we resist grows stronger.

There was very likely a projective identification here as well. As soon as she gave him the cold stare, she had become identified in his mind as the witch-mother, and he responded not to the human being beside him but to his projective identification. She saw his frightened look and his attempt to avoid her and probably felt like a witch, which may have caused her to press her foot down on his foot even harder. Perhaps her younger brother had called her a monster or witch, and so a witchlike spite lay latent in her character, ready to be aroused by the right circumstances. Hence, the emotional contagion would have been, in that sense, double-edged: His fear would have aroused her excitement and spite, and her spite would have aroused his excitement and fear.

Something similar took place during my brief treatment of Mr. Snickler. I felt Mr. Snickler's rage as soon as he walked into my office. I felt myself pulling back, trying not to let his rage get to me. He looked contemptuously at my office, at my chair, at me. I pulled back more and more, afraid of him. This was my counterresistance. I felt susceptible to him, and this aroused countertransference resistance. Throughout the treatment, I was reeling from the emotional contagion. He was an extremely contagious individual, carrying the contagion from his mother and father, from his previous therapist, and from the therapist with whom he had sparred right before coming to me.

My counterresistance was, I believe, a combination of two of the types I have described. It was a countertransference resistance in that it was, in one sense, provoked by Mr. Snickler's specific menacing of me, which tied in with events of my own childhood. It was also a cultural counterresistance in that it was influenced by my response to the feminist movement, by his resistance to that response, and by my resistance to his resistance.

Emotional contagion plays perhaps an even more dramatic role in the formation of cultural resistances and counterresistances. Any social movement will generate a certain amount of emotional contagion. During the McCarthy hearings of the early 1950s, for example, waves of fear ran through America, and this fear caused people to think differently and behave differently. Suddenly there was a new standard for judging a person's worth: it depended on whether one was loyal to America, or was a communist sympathizer. During those days, one had to watch everything one said, wrote, even thought, lest one be branded a communist. To be branded a communist meant losing all status in society and in one's community.

An older colleague who was practicing therapy then told me that when he was with patients he could almost feel the hysteria of the times in his office. He was always watching everything he said to his patients, and they were watching everything they said, lest one decide the other was a communist. He heard of cases in which patients had charged their therapists with being communists, left them, and even reported them to authorities. He remembers the face of one colleague who had been called before a professional committee and chastised. This colleague had always been contented, optimistic. Now his face was glum, bitter, muted. His emotional forcefield had been completely changed. He had been infected, by the mass anti-communist hysteria. These kinds of crusades and movements have, as I mentioned before, occurred throughout history and appear to be some kind of mass playing out of the duality of life, and of societal resistance and counterresistance.

Emotional forcefields and emotional contagion are part and parcel of psychotherapy. They fuel transference and countertransference, are at the root of splitting and projective identification, and are the mainspring of resistance and counterresistance. Without the phenomenon of emotional contagion, the therapist's task would be much easier. Perhaps this is what Freud meant when he said, "The psychoanalyst knows that the forces he works with are of the most explosive kind, and he needs as much caution and conscientiousness as a chemist" (1915, p. 390).

# 12

# The Uses of Objective Counterresistance

In a previous book (1991b) I wrote, "All resistance to therapy is, directly or indirectly, an expression of hate" (p. 15). If that is so, then all counterresistance is also an expression of hate.

These assertions are purposely simplistic in order to convey the dualism of life. It is a dualism that, in Eastern philosophy, is characterized by the symbol of yin and yang, and in psychoanalysis by Freud's concept of eros and thanatos. (See Figure 12–1.) In this simplified scheme, love is defined as a bonding with other human beings based on genuine, honest relating. Hate is anything that obstructs that bonding. What we therapists are doing, then, is teaching people how to love. However, if we ourselves have problems with getting close to, communicating with, or tolerating certain people, then we will not be able to teach our patients properly.

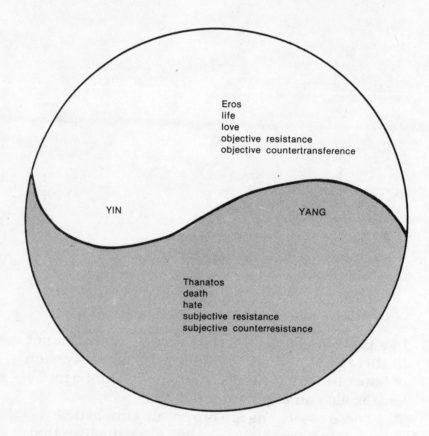

**Figure 12.1.** Dualities of Life and Therapy

In my previous book I made a distinction between objective and subjective hate, which is basi-
cally the same distinction that I made earlier in
Chapter 1 with regard to objective and subjective
countertransference and counterresistance. Up until now we have mainly described types of subjective counterresistance (or a therapist's subjective
hatred of the patient). Subjective counterresistance
always involves some unresolved, unconscious

feelings or ideas that the therapist is acting out in the therapy relationship. It may be partially induced by the patient's transference and resistance. Objective counterresistance, on the other hand, is always provoked by the patient's transference and resistance and, even though it might arouse feelings from the therapist's past, the therapist is aware of the source of these feelings and can distinguish them from what the patient is inducing. Moreover, the therapist is always conscious of objective counterresistance and expresses his "hate" for the patient in this objectified way not to hurt the patient, but to bring about love—that is, to bring about genuine bonding between himself and the patient.

A patient's transference and resistance can also be objective or subjective. Generally they are subjective, for we assume that patients are not as in touch with their unconscious as therapists are; but in those rare cases in which a patient is matched up with a therapist who is less integrated and aware than the patient, it may well be that the patient's transference and resistance are almost entirely provoked by the therapist. The patient may then feel that the therapist has wrongfully cast him as a persecuting object, and the patient may begin to experience, through introjection, impulses of persecuting the therapist (a transference resistance impulse). In such a case, leaving therapy would be an expression of objective transference and objective resistance.

Subjective resistance and counterresistance can be expressed in two ways: it can be acted out or it can be somatized. Examples of acted-out resist-

ance include anything from not speaking to somebody, to missing an appointment, to killing somebody. Examples of somatized resistance include
anything from falling asleep, to getting a headache,
to dying of a heart attack.

Probably one of the most difficult things for
therapists to master is this ability to analyze themselves and to distinguish between subjective and
objective countertransference and counterresistance. I still have not mastered it, and perhaps I
never will. One of the keys to doing it is to become
aware of your feelings, particularly your hate. Hate
in all its many forms (envy, resentment, fear) is
difficult for humans to acknowledge. "What, me
hate? Never!" This universal inclination to disavow
hate is one of humanity's most destructive tendencies. The denial and projection of hate keep hate
alive and subjective (unconscious). It seems to me
that when one can say, "Yes, I hate, and sometimes
I hate rationally and sometimes irrationally, and
I'm working on it," then one is approaching emotional responsibility.

Good therapy and supervision train therapists
to accept all of their feelings, especially their hate;
to understand what they are feeling at all times and
why; to know when those feelings are centered and
objective rather than uncentered and subjective;
and to use those feelings in making the response
that each patient requires.

## ANALYZING AND RESOLVING
## COUNTERRESISTANCE

The focus until now has been on types and manifestations of counterresistance. Obviously, before

therapists can analyze and resolve subjective counterresistance, they must learn to detect it and to understand what type it is and what its implications are. There have been allusions to the process of analyzing and resolving counterresistance throughout the book, so this will more or less be a summary.

First and foremost, the process involves keeping an eye on signs that we are counterresisting. Are we doing any of the things listed in Table 3–1 (i.e., coming late for sessions, falling asleep, talking too much or too little, avoiding eye contact, expressing things impulsively, feeling obsessed, lustful, enraged)? Such signs should serve to prompt us to begin to analyze our feelings about the case and what is arousing them.

At the same time, the process involves taking cues from the patient's resistance. Whenever we become aware of a new resistance or a variation of an old resistance, we must assume that there will be a counterresistance—or an impulse to counterresist. It is something like the law of physics that states, "Every action has an equal and opposite reaction." After we discover our own resistance, the process involves our analyzing and, if necessary, resolving it before we attempt to analyze and resolve the patient's resistance.

Analyzing our counterresistance involves, first of all, getting in touch with exactly what we are feeling. Usually, after years of training, therapists become pretty efficient at this. "Much of our work as therapists consists of identifying our feelings and understanding where they come from and what they mean," Ormont notes (1992, p. 52). To the extent we can identify and understand the meaning of our feelings we will be empowered as therapists.

Are we feeling afraid, jealous, angry? What has made us feel this way? Was it something the patient said or did? Is it something about his character or looks? Is something in our personal life affecting our relation to our patients? Is some social force affecting the therapy. Are we reacting to his transference? Is he reacting to ours? If he is making us feel this way, what does that tell us about how he sees us? If we are feeling this way, what does that tell us about how we see him?

What kind of counterresistance do we have? Is it a countertransference resistance, a characterological counterresistance, or a cultural counterresistance? Or are we unwittingly acting out some counterresistance related to the school of therapy to which we subscribe? If it is a countertransference resistance, what is it about the patient that is provoking it? If it is a characterological counterresistance, is it an ongoing repeating pattern, or has something about this situation reignited it? If it is a cultural counterresistance, from where does it stem?

Once we have analyzed the counterresistance, the process involves determining if it is subjective or objective. Often we must make this determination quickly, for we are constantly called upon to respond and make interventions based on these determinations. Yet therapy is an art, not a science, and complete objectivity is impossible. One test I have found helpful in making this determination is whether the counterresistance or impulse to counterresist is destructive or constructive to the therapeutic process. Will it facilitate bonding or destroy it? If it is destructive, then it is subjective.

A patient barges into my office and says, "I've got to use your telephone. Okay?" Without waiting for my answer he goes to the phone. He is a freelance artist and says, as he picks up the phone, that he just remembered as he walked through my door that he was supposed to call a client an hour ago. I want to tell him that he cannot use the phone but I do not. I sit silently fuming about it. I remain largely silent the rest of the session. After he leaves I ask myself whether my counterresistance (that is, my joining his resistance by allowing him to use my phone) was constructive or destructive to the therapy. Had I stopped him, he would have been enraged and might have used that as an excuse to quit therapy. He had quit before for similar reasons. By letting him go ahead and do it, I avoided taking this chance and bided my time until the next session, when he would better be able to hear about my objections to his using the phone. Also, by then I would no longer be in the heat of my feelings and would be able to discuss it calmly with him, pointing out his pattern of ramrodding me and others into doing what he wanted and guiding him toward a recognition of this pattern. In this case, therefore, my counterresistance would probably have been constructive and hence objective.

Another patient might sweetly ask to use the phone, and I may assent to it—counterresist—for the wrong reasons. I may have a mother-transference toward the patient and be needful of her approval. The patient, while professing to be grateful, senses my need for approval and loses respect for me and for the therapy process. Even if I tell her later that her using the phone is a resistance, she still senses this need for her approval. She realizes that there was no reason I could not have said no to her in the first place. She would not have quit had I done so, and in fact would have respected me more and probably even wanted to talk about it. My failure in this case was an acting out of subjective counterresistance, a response primarily to my own transference to her.

Another method of checking for subjectivity is to pay attention when patients, friends, or colleagues are repeatedly telling us things. If many are telling us the same thing, it is usually valid.

After determining that some piece of counterresistance is subjective, the process involves resolving it. Resolving counterresistance is no different than resolving the patient's resistance; it entails analysis, interpretation, and working through. Usually, experienced therapists can quickly work through the countertransference feelings behind a counterresistance because they have already done it so many times before during the course of their training therapy. Perhaps it will require a few hours or a night or perhaps even two nights. If it takes much longer, then they need to seek help in the form of feedback from colleagues, more supervision, or more therapy.

Some people advocate lifelong supervision. I still attend a supervision group comprised of advanced therapists and am not reluctant to seek therapy when I need it. Just as any machine, to be in good working order, requires ongoing maintenance, so does a therapist. A therapist's ongoing supervision is perhaps the best preventative therapy for his patients.

When we have mastered the art of identifying and understanding our countertransference and counterresistance and can distinguish between the subjective and the objective, we are ready to make use of objective counterresistance to advance therapeutic progress. Following are some examples of how I have used objective counterresistance in treating a few of my more difficult patients.

## PATIENTS WHO GO FOR THE JUGULAR

There are some difficult patients who will immediately sniff out the therapist's weaknesses, whatever they are and launch a lightning attack. Bill, a borderline patient with a strong paranoid substructure, lost no time in throwing out the gauntlet. In his first session, seated facing me, his dark eyes sizing me up, Bill suddenly asked, "Do you always nod like an idiot?" I had been listening to his story, nodding profusely, probably to ward off feelings of fear he was inducing. "I find it distracting when you nod like that," he added.

I was momentarily stunned. As he eyed me triumphantly, I checked myself out. What had happened? What was I feeling? Why had it happened? After a few moments I realized I had been blindsided, and it had left me feeling scared, angry, and idiotic. Had my nodding really been idiotic? No; it was a bit defensive, but not idiotic. Was my nodding a counterresistance? Yes, to a degree; it was a character trait, a way of defending against being rejected. However, it did not warrant the huge dose of hostility the patient had flung at me, hence it was not really responsible for his resistance, but had merely served as an excuse for his trying to destroy my sense of myself and make me feel ashamedly idiotic.

I began to nod some more, exaggeratedly, smiling very brightly at his dark eyes, and emitting a grossly idiotic noise. "Yeeeuk! . . . yeeeuk! . . ." I let him know with this exaggerated nod, smile, and noise that I hated him as much as he hated me, and that I could be truly idiotic if I felt like it, with no loss of dignity. Words were not necessary. He chuckled slightly, seemed befuddled, and looked down. Then, turning his gaze away from me, he continued his story.

It was just a brief moment in the interview, but I knew it was the pivotal one. Bill signed on as a patient, and although there were more clashes, they did not get out of hand. I had parried his first thrust and taken control of the therapy, and it was relatively easy to parry the ones after that.

I had learned that it was important with such patients to let them know from the outset that I could be as hateful as they could. If they felt they could out-hate me from the beginning, the game was over. I had lost many patients in the first interview simply because I would be reluctant to meet an initial attack that, on an emotional level, seemed as though it would require "taking arms against a sea of troubles." Blitzkriegs can stun you, and you can sense the rage behind them and feel that it is useless to confront them. So the tendency is to remain silent and hope they go away. Invariably, the patient goes away. However, if you meet the challenge, if you meet subjective resistance with objective counterresistance, you often find, as in this case, that this initial attitude is somewhat of a test or bluff. Once the patient feels your counterresistance, and realizes that it is a nonhostile, nontoxic counterresistance designed to bring about peace and bonding, the patient feels safe and understood.

## PATIENTS WHO SEDUCE

There are many kinds of seducers, from those who appeal to therapists' narcissism and try to please them to death, to those who appeal to therapists' lust and try to charm them to death.

In the first category are the devoted followers. These are the kinds of people who will attach themselves to a cult figure and do anything for that person, even kill for him. Every therapist has such individuals as patients. They may appear to be the perfect patient, bringing in dreams, free associating with zest, listening and applying the therapist's every interpretation. Often such patients either have an oral-dependent need to merge themselves to an idealized figure in order to drink in his omniscience or omnipotence; or they suffer from a schizoid lack of self, or from masochistic inferiority.

One such patient, John, seemed quite content to bask in my "glow," and might have done so for years, had I not decided to act out the counterresistance impulses I was experiencing. John would come in each session smiling at me shyly like a child, plop on the couch, and gush forth dreams, fantasies, thoughts, and feelings. He spoke often of his relationship with me and enthusiastically analyzed his transference from his parents. Months passed. Years passed. And still he continued to smile at me like a little boy each time he entered. Despite all his seemingly good therapeutic work, he remained in this state of childlike dependence.

Now and again I found myself feeling uneasy about his smile and his presence—the kind of uneasiness one feels about somebody who develops a crush on you and sighs over your every word. Even though his relationship to me was a positive transference, it was still a subjective resistance. It was resisting a real relationship and clinging to an idealizing-dependent one. After analyzing my own feelings to see if I was resisting too, I came upon a plan.

"You know," I said one day. "I think it's time we talk about termination." I had no intention of terminating. I just wanted to counterresist his resistance.

"What do you mean?" he asked. "I'm not ready to terminate."

"How come?"

"I don't know." He blushed confusedly. "I . . . need you."

"What do you need me for?"

"I need somebody to talk to."

"You can talk to friends."

"That's different."

"How?"

"They're . . . not you."

"What do you mean?"

"They don't know me the way you do."

"So you don't want to talk about termination."

"Not really."

"What's your objection to discussing termination?"

"I don't know.

"You seem to be doing better."

"Maybe not."

His face had turned dark, the smile had faded. There was, for the first time, anger in his voice. I had shaken him out of his cocoon. What he wanted was to stay in that cocoon, to remain a follower, to fill his inner emptiness with my supposed fullness, to idealize me and, in turn, be accepted and blessed by this idealized figure, so that he could continue to blissfully disown, primarily through repression, the rage that seethed deep inside him and remain in a state of childlike unconsciousness. I continued to bring up the necessity of discussing termination until one day he said, "Everybody's always pushed me away," and I said, "Tell me about it." He did, and our relationship began to change.

There are pleasers and there are charmers. Charmers can be male or female, and they use sexuality to entrance you, lull you, ingratiate you, and woo you into a state of submission. They can be relentless, and behind this charming facade is a narcissistic demandingness that, when rebuffed, can turn into hostile spite.

Melissa was a charmer who would strut into my office oozing wanton lust. "I don't know what it is," she would say in a sensual, resigned voice, lying languorously on the couch, one knee arched and revealed as her skirt fell back. "I think I must be hypersexed. I can't seem to control my urges. I seem addicted to wild sex. Is that normal?" She was a 30-year-old painter who did huge, red abstract paintings. She looked up at me with smiling brown eyes, a pouty lower lip, and large white teeth that—when my countertransference was at its zenith—appeared like fangs.

Sometimes she came bearing gifts, her eyes sparkling like Christmas lights—laying into my hands cookies that smacked of home, a little plant she had nurtured from a seedling, a book whose pages had become bent with use—and, smiling with all her teeth, she would straighten her dress and say, "I just wanted to give you something. I don't know why. I guess because you listen. God knows, my father never listened." She had an obsession with her father, who had tantalized and rejected her throughout her childhood. But she would not talk about him. Instead, she would tantalize me, give me a tiny bit of father stuff, and then resume her seduction of the therapist.

Sometimes she would up the ante by regaling me with one of her erotic dreams. "I had a dream about you last night," she would say in a matter-of-fact tone, her pouty lower lip jutting out, as though she didn't really want to tell me about it but she would if it would make me happy. "I dreamed—this is really weird—I dreamed there was this terribly large moon floating in the sky and you were walking along and you saw this moon, and then it wasn't a moon, it was a breast up there, a big orange breast, dangling just above the buildings. And then as you were looking at it, the breast began to drift down and you reached up and took it in your hand and placed it in your back pocket." She smirked at me knowingly. "Well, what do you make of it?"

"What do *you* make of it?" I quickly replied.

She struggled for at least two or three minutes to find a meaning, then gave up. "Oh, by the way," she continued in the same flip tone. "Did I tell you how I gave Max a blow job last weekend while he was driving on the turnpike. It was wild. Have you ever had a blow job while you were driving? Nah, you're probably too straightlaced for that."

Her seduction was thorough and unmitigated. If she was not giving me gifts or giving me the eye, she was telling me about each new man she had made it with in some new and different way, or about each stranger she wanted to do it with in any old way. She identified with the aggressor, her father, a militant womanizer, and she herself had become a militant manizer. There was no working alliance between us; rather, it was a working battle.

Freud noted in his paper "Observations on Transference-Love" (1915) that the erotic transference was one of the most difficult to resolve. He advised preserving it for the purposes of analysis, while neither discouraging or gratifying it. However, he added that there were some women with whom this policy would not work. "These are women of an elemental passionateness; they tolerate no surrogates; they are children of nature who refuse to accept the spiritual instead of the material; to use the poet's words, they are amenable only to the 'logic of gruel and the argument of dumplings'." With these women, Freud went on, a therapist was forced to make a choice, "Either to return their love or else bring down upon oneself the full force of the mortified woman's fury" (p. 386).

I learned from experience that Freud was right. There did not seem to be a way of resolving the erotic transferences of such women. I tried being delicate, being blunt, ignoring, rejecting, and heaping on them an array of brilliant interpretations, tracing their behavior all the way back to the womb. Nothing seemed to work. However, with Melissa, perhaps because there was a bit of a real relationship between us, I managed to turn things around.

During the course of her treatment she stopped and started several times. Her repeating pattern was to assult me with seduction and, when that failed to achieve results, to abruptly quit therapy in a sulky way, her lower lip jutting forth. "I have to quit therapy. I'm out of money. I'll call you." She always did call again in a few months or a year, after her seduction had failed with another man.

I found myself constantly feeling enraged by her. The impulse was to counterresist by kicking her out and telling her to never come back. What I did instead was to use these feelings, objectify them, and join her resistance, but without malice.

"Maybe it's best that you quit," I said the next time she spoke of quitting.

"Why?" she asked, glancing at me skeptically.

"Because I'm feeling frustrated."

"I'm sure."

"It's not what you think. I'm frustrated because we don't seem to be able to really connect with each other. What I really want to do is to form a friendly working relationship with you, but I think you think that deep down I want to have sex with you. You think that I want to form a friendly relationship in order to get you to go to bed with me, but that's not it at all. Sometimes men really *do* just want to be friends. Not all men are out to get into your pants.''

She smiled skeptically but said nothing.

For several weeks she went back to the charming routine. Then she once again spoke of quitting. However, when I persisted in joining her resistance, her skepticism changed to confusion. Had I been pretending, she would have sensed it immediately. But, in fact, I meant everything I was saying; I really did want to get rid of her, and so she became gradually convinced as well. She also came to understand that if she could resolve our conflict, she would be able to resolve similar problems in her personal relationships.

This was the turning point of the therapy. Not that it was easy after that. Melissa continued to be provocative, and I kept joining her resistance, giving her nothing to fight. Somehow we both stuck it out and she began, over the next year, to learn to hate more constructively.

## PATIENTS WHO INTIMIDATE

Jack was one of the most demanding and enraging patients ever to invade my office. I say invade because he had a way of taking over any space that he occupied, always fidgeting, always talking, always gesturing, and always keeping others at bay by saying the most provocative things and by not allowing any feedback. There were many occasions during my work with him when I had a strong urge to murder him. The major theme of his life was his demand for absolute allegience by those around him, including his therapist, a demand that he enforced through various types of intimidation, including mental torture, threats, and physical abuse. It was not just that he required me to be an idealizing selfobject (Kohut 1979); he demanded that I be a sanctifying selfobject, who would hold him and all his actions, no matter how outrageous, to be sacred and unassailable.

Jack initially sought therapy because he felt blocked as an actor, and this was where he wanted to keep the focus of the treatment—on his creative block. Meanwhile, he would let it drop, as an aside, that he had had a fight with his live-in girlfriend and had broken her jaw, or that he gotten into an altercation with a director and blackened the director's eye, or that he was stealing cash from the petty cash drawer at his job, and he would expect me to understand and agree completely with his rationalizations for doing these things. He let me know, in so many words, that if I said one discouraging word, he would be out the door.

Indeed, if I frustrated him in the slightest way, he would badger me for session after session to get me to give him what he wanted. For instance, he once asked me a personal question. When I turned the question back to him, inquiring what that information would mean to him, he shook his head and rolled back his eyes. Although he was in his late thirties and had lived a decadent life, his face glowed with the eternal innocence and optimism of an adolescent, so that I felt petty not giving in to such a meager request.

"Why won't you answer my question?" he asked.

"I've explained it to you. I don't answer personal questions because I wish to maintain a blank screen."

"That's bullshit. You're just afraid to reveal yourself to me, afraid of what I might find out about you."

"If you say so.

"Why do you have to be a blank screen?"

"I've explained it to you many times before."

"Explain it again."

"Why? You haven't remembered what I've said in the past, so you probably won't remember it this time either."

"I'll remember it this time."

"I doubt it."

"If I raise your fee will you answer my question?"

"No."

"If I start coming on time?"

"No. I would like you to come on time for your sake, not mine."

"If I get you two tickets to my play?"

"No."

"You know, you really are a jerk. You really are. It wouldn't do any harm to answer the question. You just want to torture me."

"Why would I want to do that?"

"It makes you feel clever to torture me. That's how you shrinks get off your rocks, isn't it.

Once he got onto one of these jags, it could go on for weeks. Not only would he attempt to intimidate and manipulate me during the sessions, he would also leave messages on my machine or call me at my home at an inappropriate hour and begin badgering me again about answering the question. Eventually it would lead to a showdown in which he would threaten to leave unless I answered the question, and I would tell him if that is what he wanted to do then he could do that. He would then swear at me and insult my mother and every other member of my family and then would forget all about the incident, as though it had never happened.

He rarely talked about his childhood, and when he did it was always to praise both his mother and father, regarding them as sacred objects never to be raised up to the light of objectivity. Nevertheless, what became abundantly clear to me about his childhood was that his parents had indulged their only son totally, pampered him, given him anything he asked for, and never set a limit on his behavior: In their eyes he could do no wrong, and therefore in his eyes they had done no wrong. One fact stands out in his history and demonstrates the extent of the mother's pampering. Until he left home for college, at the age of 18, his mother still wiped his behind after he emptied his bowels. Because of this pampering, my patient had developed a severely narcissistic character. He required total pampering from others, and viewed it as a narcissistic injury if anybody refused any request by him. He also had strong phallic narcissistic features that were the source of a need to conquer sexually one or two women a day. If he could not get women to sleep with him through the use of his boyish charm, he would intimidate them into doing it, and if all else failed, he would pay a prostitute and degrade her in order to extract his conquest. His relationships with men were tinged with oedipal guilt, as he had usurped his passive father's position in the family triangle. It was the oedipal guilt that made it possible for him to relate to a male therapist with any success at all, for it aroused in him a need to appease me.

From the outset I felt conflicted about how to deal with him. If I became the sanctifying selfobject he wanted me to be, he would stay in therapy with me, and maybe, just maybe, at some distant point down the road he would begin to look at himself on his own. However, in the meantime, I had to bear witness to his tales of physical abuse, stealing, and manipulation of others, as well as tolerate a good deal of abuse from him myself, such as his telephoning me at odd hours. Eventually, my countertransference anger became so large that it was affecting my capacity to empathize with him. I had analyzed myself to determine if I had in some way contributed to his acting out through a counterresistance of my own. But I had not. It was clearly his characteristic pattern. Before me he had already dumped several other therapists. What I decided to do was simply to be honest about the way he was making me feel. So, one day I told him, "You know, sometimes I want to kill you." I said it without raising my voice.

"Why do you want to kill me?" he finally asked, in a perplexed, little-boy voice. He told me later that he was shocked. He had never in his conscious mind imagined that he could be a hateful person, although on an unconscious level he had known it all along and was seeking a confirmation of it through his provocative behavior. In his conscious mind he saw only his ideal image of himself, the image his mother had seen, the charming young prince who was a bit devilish, but not devilish enough to be concerned about. This was a minor turning point of his therapy, one that put a little chink in his armor and allowed me to continue working with him without strangling him. By expressing my hate purely without condemning him, I precluded his responding with any of his usual defenses. Had I tried to talk to him, interpret his behavior, manipulate him, or make up new rules to control his behavior, he would have viewed that as provocation and would have stepped up his acting out or left therapy. One cannot defend against a pure verbal expression of direct hate that is delivered at the proper time. One can only feel it. In addition, my direct expression of hate served as a model for him, demonstrating how to have an authentic relationship in which feelings are expressed directly rather than acted out. Because he perceived that his mother and father would have had heart attacks if he had ever expressed any direct anger to them, he had grown up thinking that the only way to express anger was to act it out in ways people could not rebuff. My direct expression of objective hate was the antidote to his acting out of subjective hate.

## PATIENTS WHO ARE SILENT

Silence can mean many things, but it is nearly always a resistance—probably the most common of all. When patients are silent, my impulse is to counterresist with silence or to prod them into speaking. I feel impatient, annoyed, and deprived, and stubbornly want to deprive them back or attack their stubbornness. However, I have learned that neither tactic works; what generally does work is if I ask object oriented questions.

"May I ask you a question?" I may say.

"Sure."

"I'm puzzled by your silence. I'm wondering if I've done anything to cause you to be silent."

"I don't know. Maybe I want you to say more."

"Oh, so you're feeling deprived by me?"

"Maybe."

This usually gets patients to communicate what the silence is about. It tells them that I am interested in their opinion and willing to listen to what they have to say and even to change my behavior for them if necessary. This takes the onus of change off them and onto me. In other cases I might try a different approach.

"Tell me something. When you're silent, should I just let you be silent or should I say something?"

"You should say something."

"What should I say?"

"I don't know. You're the therapist."

"You want me to guess what needs to be said at that moment."

"I suppose."

"What if I'm not smart enough to guess what to say?"

"I'd be annoyed."

"And if I guess the right thing?"

"I'd feel understood."

Again, by involving the patient in the exploring of my own behavior, he or she has been induced to communicate and explore.

Some analysts are prone to getting locked in a silence-versus-silence power struggle with patients. I have heard of cases in which nothing was said for months. This is totally unnecessary and is simply a case of the therapist's counterresistance impulses being acted out rather than being used to understand the patient's feelings. On the other hand, some therapists will attempt to persuade the patient to talk by making empathic statements such as, "I suppose you must feel terrible right now." This usually does not work because the patient feels intruded upon as he once did by his parents. Such statement are heard as demands to speak, not as real empathy.

## STAYING IN TUNE WITH THE PATIENT

Real empathy means staying in tune with patients and giving them what they need—whether that be a statement of sympathy, or a confrontation of their acting out. The key to using objective counterresistance is to stay in tune, always being willing to meet patients at their level. It is not up to patients to attune themselves to the therapist, but rather for therapists to stay attuned with patients by paying attention to the kinds of fantasies, thoughts, feelings, and impulses the patients induce in them.

One silent patient may induce rage in the therapist, another may induce pity, lust, or fear. Each of these emotional responses to the patient's silence reveals something different about what is going on in the transference and what went on in the patient's past. Each requires a different intervention.

Moreover, each form of silence may involve a different kind of projection or projective identification. In one case, the therapist may feel as though he were a monster from whom the patient must protect himself; in another, a maternal, rescuing angel, with impulses to smother the patient with kindness; in another, a sexual conquistador with desires of ravishing the patient; in another, a helpless child waiting in terror for a parent's violence to erupt. None of these attitudes represents who the therapist really is.

By objectifying these induced and projected attitudes and feelings, the therapist can understand what the silence is about and the kinds of resistance and counterresistance that went on in the patient's childhood. If the patient's silence induces feelings of rage and makes the therapist feel like a monster who wants to crush the patient, then this will help the therapist understand that there must have been a monster in the patient's early childhood from whom he had to hide. It may also mean that the patient harbors a monstrous side from which the therapist must be protected.

Likewise with all other forms of resistance—ranging from lateness to seductiveness and from babbling to shouting—each can have many different meanings and can require many different kinds of interventions. Each also may signal the existence of many different kinds of counterresistance to which the therapist must pay attention.

The specter of counterresistance is always there. If we are unaware, it will sabotage all we try to do. If we are aware, it can become a crucial tool.

I am reminded of a tale told by Chuang Tzu. The Prince of Wu took a hunting party on a boat to Monkey Hill. When the monkeys saw the Prince and his men, they darted frantically to the tops of the trees. One monkey, however, did not run off, but kept swinging from branch to branch, quite calmly, as though showing off for the Prince. The Prince shot an arrow at this monkey, and the monkey deftly caught it in his hand. Dismayed, the Prince then ordered his men to shoot the monkey down. In an instant the monkey was full of arrows. It gasped in bewilderment and fell to the ground.

The Prince turned to his companion, Yen Pui, and said, "You see what happened? This monkey flaunted his cleverness. He was conceited about his abilities. He thought that nobody could come near him. Always remember: It is those things about us that stand out, and of which we are not aware, that will cause us problems."

When they returned to their hometown, Yen

Pui began studying with a local Taoist sage in order to rid himself of everything that made him stand out. He gave up every desire and let go of all of his claims of superiority.

After three years no one in the town could figure him out.

So they admired him.

# References

Balint, M. (1968). *The Basic Fault*. London: Tavistock.

Bateson, G., Jackson, D. D., Haley, J. and Weakland, J. M. (1981). Towards a theory of schizophrenia. In *Family Therapy*, ed. by R. J. Green and J. L. Framo. New York: International Universities Press.

Benedict, R. (1934). *Patterns of Culture*. New York: Mentor.

Blum, H. (1980). The borderline childhood of the Wolf Man. In *Freud and His Patients*, ed. M. Kanzer & J. Glenn, pp. 341–358. Northvale, NJ: Jason Aronson.

Breuer, J. and Freud, S. (1893–95). Studies on hysteria. *Standard Edition*: 2. London: Hogarth, 1955.

Brill, A. A. (1949). *Basic Principles of Psychoanalysis*. Garden City, NY: Doubleday.

Chagnon, N. A. (1968). *Yanamamö: The Fierce People*. New York: Holt, Rinehart & Winston.

Eissler, K. R. (1953). The effect of the structure of the ego in psycho-analytic technique. *Journal of the American Psychoanalytic Association* 1:104–143.

Escalona, S. (1953). Emotional development in the first year of life. In *Problems of Infancy and Childhood*, trans. by M. Senn. Ann Arbor, MI: Josiah Macy, Jr. Foundation.

Estabrooks, G. H. (1943). *Hypnotism*. New York: Dutton, 1957.

Ferenzci, S. (1930). The principles of relaxation and neocatharsis. *Final Contributions to the Theory and Technique of Psycho-Analysis*, ed. M. Balint, trans. E. Mosbacher. New York: Basic Books.

_____ (1933). Confusion of tongues between adults and the child. In *Further Contributions to the Theory and Technique of Psycho-Analysis*, compiled by J. Rickman, trans. J. I. Suttee. pp. 156–167. New York: Brunner/Mazel, 1980.

Ferenzci, S., and Rank, O. (1925). *The Development of Psychoanalysis*. New York: Nervous and Mental Disease Publishing Co.

Flournay, H. (1927). A report on a case of folie à deux. *Swiss Archives of Neurology and Psychiatry*, 20:44–55.

Freud, A. (1936). *The Ego and the Mechanisms of Defense*. New York: International Universities Press, 1946.

Freud, S. (1900). *The Interpretation of Dreams. Standard Edition* 4 and 5.

_____ (1905). Fragment of an analysis of a case of hysteria. *Standard Edition* 7:3–124.

_____ (1909). Notes upon a case of obsessional neurosis. *Standard Edition.* 10:153–318.

_____ (1910). The future prospects of psychoanalytic therapy. *Standard Edition*, 11:139–151.

_____ (1912). The dynamics of transference. *Standard Edition*, 12:97–108.

_____ (1914). Remembering, repeating, working through. *Standard Edition*, 2:145–156.

_____ (1915). Further recommendations in the technique of psycho-analysis: observations on transference-love. *Standard Edition*, 12:157–174.

_____ (1916–1917). introductory lectures on psychoanalysis. *Standard Edition*, 15/16:313–340.

_____ (1918). From the history of an infantile neurosis. *Standard Edition*, 17:1–124.

_____ (1920). Beyond the pleasure principle. *Standard Edition*, 18:3–66.

_____ (1926). Inhibitions, symptoms, and anxiety. *Standard Edition*, 20:77–175.

_____ (1937). Analysis terminable and interminable. *Standard Edition*, 23:209–253.

Fromm, E., Suzuki, D. T., and DeMartino, R. (1960). *Zen Buddhism and Psychoanalysis.* New York: Harper & Row.

Fromm-Reichmann, F. (1950). *The Principles of Intensive Psychotherapy.* Chicago: Phoenix.

Gill, M. M. (1982). *Analysis of the Transference*, vol. 1: Theory and Technique. New York: International Universities Press.

Glover, E. (1955). *The Technique of Psycho-Analysis*. New York: International Universities Press.

Greenson, R. R. (1967). *The Technique and Practice of Psychoanalysis*, vol. 1. New York: International Universities Press.

_____ (1978). *Explorations in Psychoanalysis*. New York: International Universities Press.

Hartmann, H. (1950). *Essays on Ego Psychology*. New York: International Universities Press.

Jung, C. G. (1935). Principles of practical psychotherapy. *Collected Works of C. G. Jung*, vol. 16. Princeton, NJ: Princeton University Press.

_____ (1971). *The Portable Jung*, ed. by J. Campbell. New York: Viking.

Kanefield, L. (1985). Psychoanalytic constructions of female development and women's conflicts about achievement. *Journal of the American Academy of Psychoanalysis* 13:347–366.

Kanzer, M. (1980). The transference neurosis of the Rat Man. In *Freud and His Patients*, ed. by M. Kanzer and J. Glenn, pp. 137–144. Northvale, NJ: Jason Aronson.

Kernberg, O. E., Selzer, M. A., Koenigsberg, H. W., et al. (1989). *Psychodynamic Psychotherapy of Borderline Patients*. New York: Basic Books.

Klein, M. (1932). *The Psycho-Analysis of Children*, trans. J. Strachey. New York: Delacorte, 1975.

Kohut, H. (1971). *The Analysis of the Self*. New York: International Universities Press.

_____ (1978). Narcissism as a resistance and as a driving force in psychoanalysis. In *The Search for the Self*, vol. II, ed. P. Ornstein, pp. 547–562. New York: International Universities Press.

_____ (1979). The two analyses of Mr. Z. *International Journal of Psycho-Analysis* 60:3–27.

Laing, R. D. (1971). *The Politics of the Family*. Harmondsworth, England: Penguin.

Langs, R. (1980). The misalliance dimension in the case of the Wolf Man. In *Freud and His Patients*, ed. M. Kanzer & J. Glenn, pp. 215–231. Northvale, NJ: Jason Aronson.

Little, M. (1981). *Transference Neurosis and Transference Psychosis*. Northvale, NJ: Jason Aronson.

Marshall, R. J. (1991). Comparisons, contrasts and convergences. *Modern Psychoanalysis* 16: 25–34.

McDougall, W. (1920). *The Group Mind*. Cambridge: The Cambridge University Press.

Meyerson, P. (1981). The nature of transactions that occur in other than classical analysis. *International Review of Psycho-Analysis* 8:177–189.

Milgram, S. (1974). *Obedience to Authority*. New York: Harper & Row.

Miller, A. (1984). *Thou Shalt Not Be Aware: Society's Betrayal of the Child*. Trans. by H. and H. Hannum. New York: Farrar, Straus, Giroux.

Ormont, L. (1992). *The Group Therapy Experience*. New York: St. Martin's Press.

Racker, H. (1968). *Transference and Countertransference*. New York: International Universities Press.

Rado, S. (1953). Recent advances in psychoanalytic therapy. In *Psychoanalysis of Behavior*, pp. 151–167. New York: Grune & Stratton, 1957.

Reich, W. (1933). *Character Analysis*, 3rd Ed. Trans. U. R. Carfagno. New York: Pocket Books, 1973.

Roback, A. A. and Kiernan, R. (1969). *Pictorial History of Psychology and Psychiatry*. New York: Philosophical Library.

Robertiello, R. and Schoenewolf, G. (1987). *101 Common Therapeutic Blunders*. Northvale, NJ: Jason Aronson.

Rosenfeld, E. (1956). Dream and vision. *International Journal of Psycho-Analysis*, 3:97–105.

Schneiderman, S. (1980). *Returning to Freud: Clinical Psychoanalysis in the School of Lacan*. New Haven, CT: Yale University Press.

Schoenewolf, G. (1989). *Sexual Animosity between Men and Women*. Northvale, NJ: Jason Aronson.

———— (1991a). *Turning Points in Analytic Therapy: From Winnicott to Kernberg*. Northvale, NJ: Jason Aronson.

———— (1991b). *The Art of Hating*. Northvale, NJ: Jason Aronson.

Searles, H. (1979). *Countertransference and Related Subjects*. New York: International Universities Press.

Seinfeld, J. (1990). *The Bad Object*. Northvale, NJ: Jason Aronson.

Shengold, L. L. (1979). Child abuse and deprivation: soul murder. *Journal of the American Psychoanalytic Association* 17:533–560.

Shepard, M. (1972). *A Psychiatrist's Head*. New York: Dell.

Spotnitz, H. (1976). *Psychotherapy of Preoedipal Conditions* Northvale, NJ: Jason Aronson.

____ (1985). *Modern Psychoanalysis of the Schizo-phrenic Patient.* New York: Human Sciences.

Spotnitz, H., and Meadow, P. W. (1976). *Treatment of the Narcissistic Neuroses.* New York: Manhattan Center for Advanced Psychoanalytic Studies.

Stern, P. J. (1976). *The Haunted Prophet.* New York: Braziller.

Stolorow, R. D. and Atwood, G. E. (1979). *Faces in a Cloud: Subjectivity in Personality Theory.* Northvale, NJ: Jason Aronson.

Thompson, C. (1950). *Psychoanalysis: Evolution and Development.* New York: Grove.

Winnicott, D. W. (1965). *Through Paediatrics to Psycho-Analysis.* New York: Basic Books, 1975.

# Index

subtle varieties of, 92–97

summary table of, 60, 96

Wolf Man case, 78–82

Characterological resistance, category of, 13

Chou (Zhou) Dynasty, 23

Christianity. *See* Religion

Chuang Tzu, 23, 26, 28, 30, 31, 35–36, 278

Collusion, cultural counterresistance and, 106–113

Compulsion repetition, transference neurosis and, 177–178

Confrontation, suicide and, 144

Confucius, 14–15, 21, 22, 23, 24

Counterresistance emotional contagion and, 242–249

group therapy and, 157–173. *See also* Group therapy

objective counterresistance, 253–279. *See also* Objective counterresistance

research on, xiii, 11–12

resolution of, by doing nothing, 33–36

Snickler case, 199–223

symptoms of, 39–51

Taoism and, 23–24

theoretical perspective, 123–126

overview of, 123–126

psychoanalysis and (modern), 141–154

psychoanalysis (classical) and, 127–133

self psychology, 134–141

transference neurosis and, 177–196. *See also* Transference neurosis

types of, 60

Countertransference authority and, 124–125

Id, resistance and, 10
Instinct theory, 216
Integration, of patient
    parts,
    countertransference
    resistance, 69–72
Interpretation
  character defenses
      and, 23
  characterological
      counterresistance
      and, 76, 89
  of dreams,
      characterological
      counterresistance
      and, 86–87
Intimacy, resistance to,
    5–6
Intimidating patients,
    objective
    counterresistance,
    269–275


Jones, J., 233
Jung, C. G., 11, 25,
    82–87, 134


Kanefield, L., 118
Kanzer, M., 186
Kernberg, O., 240
Kiernan, R., 230, 231
Klein, M., 55, 206

Kohut, H., 46, 95, 123,
    124, 127–133, 180,
    270


Lacan, J., 113–116
Laing, R. D., 208
Langs, R., 80
Lao Tzu, 15, 21, 22, 23,
    24, 26, 27, 28, 29,
    30, 31, 32, 33, 34,
    35, 41, 97
Love
  hate and, 253
  transference neurosis
      and, 194–196
  witchcraft and,
      232–233


Marshall, R. J., 95
Masochism
  characterological
      counterresistance
      and, 87–92
  counterresistance and,
      129–130
  cultural
      counterresistance
      and, 104
McCarthy, J., 105, 106,
    248
McDougall, W., 235
Media, emotional
    contagion and, 233

Memory,
    countertransference
    resistance and,
    58–59, 70–72
Mencius, 23
Mental illness, Taoism
    and, 27
Mesmer, F. A., 232
Meyerson, P., 131
Milgram, S., 124. 125
Miller, A., 208
Mixed signals,
    counterresistance
    and, 44–45
Mo Tzu, 23
Murder, Snickler case
    and, 208, 211, 212

Narcissism
  characterological
      counterresistance
      and, 95
  cultural
      counterresistance
      and, 104
  group therapy and,
      162
  resistance and, 11
  self psychology and,
      134–135
  Taoism and, 29
Nazism, 105, 235
Negative transference,
    Reich and, 88–89

Neutrality, Taoism and,
    30

Objective
    counterresistance,
    253–279
  analyzing and
      resolving,
      256–261
  difficult patients,
      261–263
  empathy and,
      276–279
  intimidating patients,
      269–275
  overview of, 253–256
  seductive patients,
      263–269
  silent patients,
      275–276
Objective resistance,
    category of, 13
Obsessive-compulsives
  characterological
      counterresistance
      and, 80–81
  psychoanalysis and,
      124
Obsessive neurosis, Rat
    Man case and, 181
Oedipus complex
  Freud and, 186–187
  Snickler case and,
      211, 213